FERDINAND "JELLY ROLL" MORTON

FAR

FERDINAND "JELLY ROLL" MORTON

The Collected Piano Music

James Dapogny

Smithsonian Institution Press
Washington D.C.

G. SCHIRMER, *Inc.*

Distributed by
HL Hal Leonard Publishing Corporation
7777 West Bluemound Road P.O. Box 13819 Milwaukee, WI 53213

This edition is dedicated with love to my parents, Evelyn and Irving Dapogny, for their years of unfailing encouragement and practical help with music and everything else.

James Dapogny

The Smithsonian Institution wishes to thank the Estate of Anita Ford and Mrs. Hattie Holloway, Administratrix of the Estate of Anita Ford for their help in the publication of this work.

ISBN 0-87474-351-6

Reg. No. 48303c

Ed. 3257

ACKNOWLEDGMENTS

Two people have been indispensable in the realization of this project.

The first is Martin Williams, Director of the Jazz Program of the Smithsonian Institution's Division of Performing Arts. He is probably the first person to have written sensitively and accurately, from an enormous aesthetic-historical background, about Morton's music. This volume is a project that he initiated, both conceiving the idea and doing the basic work necessary to make it possible. Not only did he set this project in motion; he has also assisted greatly throughout its progress toward completion.

The second is my wife, Gail; without her help I would not have undertaken this project. She used her musical ear and years of training in checking every note of every transcription and in reading every word, spending nearly as much time on this project as I did.

Another important contributor is Michael Montgomery, who lent me his copies of the original Morton rolls from which the piano-roll transcriptions were made, and who also placed at my disposal the results of his own researches.

Jon Newsom, head of the Reference Section of the Music Division of the Library of Congress, was unstinting in helping me in the research of the printed sources of Morton's music.

I wish also to acknowledge gratefully the support of my research at the Library of Congress by a Faculty Research Grant from the Horace H. Rackham School of Graduate Studies of the University of Michigan.

Last, without being able to acknowledge their individual contributions, I want to thank the following who have all been helpful: John Clough, Richard Crawford, Gordon Darrah, Peter Ferran, Lawrence Gushee, Tony Hagert of Vernacular Music Research, Dick Hyman, Wayne Jones, Rod McDonald, Hal Smith, and Richard "Butch" Thompson.

FOREWORD

This volume undertakes a task never before undertaken: a scholarly, complete edition of a body of a jazz musician's work. It contains a version of every piece Jelly Roll Morton ever published or recorded as a piano solo.

For such a project there is little tradition of method or procedure, and so I have explained in some detail below what I have done in organization, notation, and other editorial practice.

I began my own music career as a composer, music theorist, and teacher largely because of my early interest—formed when I had already had some musical education—in the handful of Morton recordings that I could then find. My attempts to come to grips with the technical problems involved in understanding the music on those recordings led me to academic training and new musical interests, as well as to continued involvement in jazz.

The study of music of all types has only increased my admiration for Morton's work; the minor shortcomings newly discovered have always been more than offset by newly found beauties of detail and structure. Morton's music has vitality, originality, variety, and—especially noteworthy in jazz composition—coherence, qualities which are prized in the music of any good composer. In addition, on his recordings, we hear Morton the improvisor, with his unique ability to spin out variations that are simultaneously free and beautifully disciplined. Morton's is a music of substance, and greater familiarity with it brings sustained interest and greater admiration for the talents of its creator.

J.D.

CONTENTS

LIST OF ILLUSTRATIONS

Following Page 36:

A selection of Morton publication covers

Wolverine Blues, 1923, Melrose. Piano-vocal sheet music edition issued at about the time of Morton's arrival in Chicago.

Jelly Roll Blues, 1915, Rossiter. Piano sheet-music edition.

King Porter Stomp, 1925, Melrose. Piano sheet-music edition.

Blues and Stomps, 1927 (?), Melrose. Folio collecting several pieces earlier published individually.

Following Page 260:

Morton wearing his bandleader's clothes at Crystal Beach, Ontario, August, 1927. (Photo previously unpublished.)

Morton, time and place unknown. (Photo previously unpublished.)

Cannonball Blues, 1926, Melrose. Cover of the piano sheet-music edition. (Library of Congress E645852.)

Jungle Blues, 1927, Melrose. Cover of the piano sheet-music edition. (Library of Congress E665813.)

Grandpa's Spells, 1923. The Melrose edition, prepared from this or a similar copy, corrects misspellings and other irregularities but introduces mistakes of its own, including a mistaken bass line in [B]. Measures 1 and 2 of [A] show Morton's practice, in notating and playing music, of occasionally placing the melody as the lowest notes in the right hand. (Library of Congress E570417.)

Frog-I-More-Rag, 1918. The earliest copyright deposit in Morton's hand. It shows the piece very much as Morton was to record it six years later. (Library of Congress E439269.)

London Blues, 1923. Morton added the ending in pencil, apparently in 1938 when examining these manuscripts with Alan Lomax. (Library of Congress E569713.)

Ham and Eggs, 1928. Morton's manuscript of **Big Foot Ham** under a new title. The "By Jelly Roll Morton" is not in Morton's hand. Alan Lomax's transcription of Morton's comment is at the lower right. (Library of Congress E688478.)

Following Page 292:

Morton, right, and unidentified companion, apparently in California. (Photo previously unpublished.)

Morton, right, and unidentified companion, apparently in California, 1920. (Photo previously unpublished.)

Mr. Jelly Lord, 1923. A voice and piano version of the piece with no words provided. This is texturally thinner than most Morton scores and contains more notational errors. (Library of Congress E570415.)

Sporting House Rag, 1939. The stamped registry date indicates that Morton submitted this just before he recorded the piece, a recomposition of **Perfect Rag.** In the manuscript, measure 6 of [A] is missing, and in performance Morton omitted measures 15-20 in [B-1] and measures 13-14 in [B-2]. (Library of Congress E209912.)

Kansas City Stomp, 1923. Instrumental indications like those found here are fairly common in Morton's piano scores. (Library of Congress C1E570148.)

State and Madison, 1926. (Library of Congress C1E643539.)

The Pearls, 1923. Despite several errors and misspellings — some of which were reproduced in the Melrose edition — this is one of Morton's most carefully prepared early versions of his own music, and shows an intriguing mixture of sophistication and naiveté in the use of notation. (Library of Congress E570416.)

The Crave, 1939. Another late manuscript, this one lacks measure 15 of [C]. (Library of Congress C1Eunpub209909.)

Mr. Joe, 1939. This manuscript, like those of **Sporting House Rag** and **The Crave,** shows Morton's later notational practice, more fluid, with smaller characters and more accurate. There is an error though: the eighth measure of [B] is missing. (Library of Congress C1Eunpub203985.)

“JELLY ROLL” MORTON

COMPOSER

THE COMPOSER

At its simplest, jazz composition is merely the construction of harmonic patterns that are the bases for improvisation. At its most complex, it is the construction of pieces that are specific in details of harmony, instrumentation, texture, melody, and overall form, and that in addition provide for the inclusion of improvisation.

Morton is one of the very few composers who have written the latter type of piece. He was the first great jazz composer, the first to combine successfully and consistently completely predetermined elements with a provision for improvisation. Only a few other jazz musicians have worked on this plane. The obvious example, and nearest to Morton in time, is the great Duke Ellington. (One of the many sad facts about Morton's life is that he and Ellington found nothing to admire about each other, probably for reasons that have little to do directly with music.)

The most ambitious jazz composition is more than just the creation of good melodies and good arrangements (though the importance of these, and their master practitioners, should not be overlooked). It embodies these, but makes additional demands of integration and balance of components and of long-range coherence.

Although a thorough analytical discussion of Morton's music is not possible here, some important features should be mentioned. (Basic analytical commentary on most of the pieces will be found in the individual essays introducing them.)

Morton had a variety of melodic styles, ranging from the near-traditional blues style of *New Orleans Blues* to the elegant, long-lined melodic style of the third strain of *The Pearls.* The differences between these styles illustrate the diversity of influence and conception in Morton's style.

In much of Morton's work, contrast of melodic styles within a piece is used. For instance, the romantic melody of the first strain* of *Shreveport Stomp* is contrasted with the distinctive, strangely harmonized, fast-moving, chromatic melodic line of the second strain, and the slower-moving melody of the third strain, constructed as a basis for the improvisation featured on all of Morton's recordings of this piece.

In his melodies, Morton often used a system of interior repetitions of melodic or rhythmic ideas, sometimes placing them at irregular intervals.

*This term and all others marked with asterisks are defined in the Glossary, page 507.

Repetition of motivic material is obvious throughout such a melody as that of the last strain of *Frog-I-More Rag.* But the interior repetitions of the first strain of *Kansas City Stomp,* whose sixteen measures contain the same figure in the third, fifth, seventh, and eleventh measures, are less obvious because they are less pervasive. Morton used a similar system among, as well as within, melodies, as in *Big Foot Ham* (which is discussed in detail in its introductory essay). He extended the system to the use of whole phrases as well, as in *London Blues,* each of whose choruses* ends with the same phrase.

There is hardly a Morton instrumental piece which does not contain contrasts of texture as part of its composition. Morton's comments on his music, as well as some of his notations, show that he often thought of the jazz-band performance possibilities of his compositions. He used several means for varying texture: changing left-hand techniques (note, for instance, the difference between the two choruses on the last strain of *Stratford Hunch*), introducing both composed and improvised breaks, and, most important structurally, varying the number and type of melodic lines making up a texture. For example, *Grandpa's Spells* has a first strain whose principal linear content is in its melody: it has, for the most part, a purely functional, nonlinear bass line. This is contrasted with a second strain which has not only a simpler melody but also an accompanying part, the bass line, which has real linear identity. (The last strain does not expand the texture to three lines as does, for instance, the last strain of *Stratford Hunch*. It introduces variety in another way.)

All of the foregoing, even without consideration of harmonic vocabulary, harmonic rhythm, tempo, and phrase and strain length, point to resources of considerable variety. A final consideration is that Morton varied these elements independently of each other and at different rates. It is important to recognize these varieties of compositional procedure in the light of the apparent sameness of formal schemes in his music.

In terms of the broadest categories of formal design, the pieces in this volume belong to only three types: three-strain pieces, two-strain pieces, and composed variations on one strain — including the blues* pieces as a subgroup. This is only an apparent lack of variety: within these possibilities, Morton's pieces have very different shapes because of the differences in relationships among the strains and the differences in their content. One need look at only *Kansas City Stomp, The Pearls, The Crave, King Porter Stomp,* and *Big Foot Ham* to see the diversity of overall shapes possible within a realization of the three-strain scheme, the scheme Morton used most often. (Two points concerning form arise here. First, one should not be surprised that pieces in the same "form" are different. Such similar pieces in the art-music tradition are different too, and for the same reason: it is the content and order, the balance and proportion of the parts — elements that the composer controls — which give pieces their identity and individuality. Second, there are three-strain pieces, jazz pieces and others, before and after Morton's very successful ones, which do not have convincing overall shapes. The three-strain scheme Morton used so often is neither a barrier to nor a guarantee of success.)

The strains of two-strain pieces often have relative structural significance like that of the verse* and chorus* of many popular-music pieces: that is, one strain is distinctly less important than the other; often it is played only once in a performance of a piece (if it is played at all). *Jelly Roll Blues* and *Black Bottom Stomp* are exceptions. They are two-strain pieces whose first strains have composed variations and whose second strains, according to Morton's recordings of them, are designed for improvisation. In these pieces each strain is distinctive and important.

Hyena Stomp and *Jungle Blues,* discussed in their respective introductory essays, are both composed sets of variations. They are interesting because they are constructed from such small amounts of material.

Morton referred to *New Orleans Blues* as "one of the first blues as a playable composition." His concept of turning jazz music's blues from only a standard twelve-measure pattern for a player's improvisation into a composition with ordered parts and content is the idea behind this work, *Jelly Roll Blues,* and *London Blues.* These pieces are similarly constructed, each with composed variations and interior repetitions, and each using the twelve-measure blues as its only chorus structure. The remaining two blues pieces, *Dead Man Blues* and *Cannonball Blues,* are not as well developed as compositions (at least in their published forms). Perhaps this is because *Dead Man Blues* originated as a song, almost a novelty piece, and because *Cannonball Blues* is a collaborative composition. But both pieces made fine vehicles for band performances on recordings because of Morton's expansion and ordering of their materials.

(This might be the place to mention Morton's notational skill. One occasionally reads or hears that Morton could not read or notate music. That this is not so is shown by an item as early as his 1918 copyright deposit manuscript of *Frog-I-More Rag.* It is complete and accurate even with the rough-and-ready approach to note-spelling typical of much early and some later jazz notation. Morton's later manuscripts show a greater ease with notation and a greater sophistication in its use, probably because he had by then written so many piano scores, lead sheets, and jazz-band arrangements.)

Since so much of the foregoing has to do with composition — what is predetermined in a piece — the role of improvisation in Morton's music should be considered.

Morton felt that improvisation, for the most part, should take the form of varying the melody, which implies that the melody must be strong enough to warrant such treatment. In his statement, "My theory is to never discard the melody," Morton has summed up the attitude of the earlier New Orleans jazz musician. And he has also expressed his concern as composer for the piece: he did not want the melody and larger shape of a piece to be lost to the immediate aims of improvisation. It is clear that the always-varied repetition of whole sections and smaller segments is a major organizational principle in Morton's music. This is the reason for his repeated use of only a few compositional schemes that lend themselves to this compositional method and to his performing style.

In building performances by improvisation based on melodic variation, Morton adhered to ideas which seemed old-fashioned or incomprehensible to New York musicians in the late 1920s and early 1930s. They had developed their own different but equally valid ideas about the nature and role of improvisation in jazz. The dominant principle was then, and is now, that improvisation was to be based almost entirely on harmony, that a piece's harmonic pattern was all that an improvising player referred to. This is a natural step in styles increasingly dependent upon popular music for repertoire; some of it is melodically undistinguished, but all of it has workable harmonic progressions. (The new style also placed improvisation differently within a performance, tending to reserve it to only certain parts within a performance, and often placing it very effectively so as to contrast with or to be accompanied by, obviously arranged, powerful section-writing.)

Morton could and did improvise in the modern way when it was necessary. But his ideal was still melodic variation. His compositions with multiple strains and his performing style provided the variety that made this effective: melodic statements were perhaps never unadorned, and improvisation — in Morton's restricted version of it — was pervasive. Variety came through the diversity of material in the strains and the textural contrasts which were a composed part of the piece. Morton himself was capable of improvising remarkable melodic variation. Some of his finest, most exciting, recordings, for instance *Frog-I-More Rag* and *Kansas City Stomp,* show how effective this could be.

The opportunity for improvisation, in fact the necessity for it, and by implication even indications for the *kind* of improvisation to take place, is composed into a Morton piece.

Finally, Morton's influence as a composer should be considered. His pieces were fairly widely recorded and must have been even more widely played in public. This meant something different from the playing of, for example, George Gershwin's music. More than most composers of popular music, Gershwin wrote music with specific, repeatable details (in addition to melody and harmony), particularly the counterlines which emerge from (or, probably more accurately, generate) his always-interesting harmony. Even so, the specificity of a piece such as Gershwin's *Someone To Watch Over Me,* played almost always with the descending lines which emerge from the harmony, or his *Liza,* with its ascending lines, is not as great as that of, for instance, Morton's *King Porter Stomp.*

The difference is that such a piece as *King Porter Stomp* imposes upon the player a more particular way of thinking about repetition and phrase structure. This, in a general way, is how Morton's influence enters the mainstream of jazz: choosing a Morton piece to perform means, automatically, choosing a formal scheme, a rather narrow set of possibilities for an arrangement, and a set of assumptions about repetition, phrasing, and key relationships. The ideas in the piece itself and the discipline of conforming to the piece's requirements cannot help entering into a sensitive player's view of music and influencing his thinking about what is musically possible.

Morton's influence spread in another less direct way, too, by way of jazz's tradition of making new pieces from old ones. Morton himself spoke of *King Porter Stomp*'s having become the basis for other pieces, which is literally true. But he need not have stopped there, for echoes of other of his pieces also appear in jazz's repertoire, even in recent years.

In all of these pieces, Morton's fine sense of detail, order, and balance come through. In the best pieces we see why Morton can truly be considered a jazz *composer,* and why he is one of so few who can.

PIANIST

THE PIANIST

In developing his own style, Morton altered the ragtime stylistic usages he had inherited, and absorbed other influences. His departure from the ragtime style is more radical than the surface of his playing might suggest. He certainly made a more decisive break with ragtime than many of his eastern contemporaries: his insistence on a strongly melodic style (the melody strongly played, very often in octaves), near-total abandonment of eighth-note figuration, and his more elaborate and irregular bass lines show this. In this regard, Morton's playing is closer conceptually to that of Earl Hines, by making the pianist's right hand a strongly accented single voice, at times almost like that of a horn.

Morton was an excellent pianist with a smooth, regular technique, a fineness of touch that was not common among pianists of the 1920s, with a strength and a rhythmic grace that was not, and still is not, common.

He did not have the same kind of brilliant surface technique that contemporaries such as James P. Johnson had, but his music, unlike theirs, did not have a built-in requirement for it. It is easy to see how his style, using a narrower span of the keyboard, a usually less brilliant-sounding right-hand style, and a complicated left-hand style, could seem less accomplished, even more primitive, to the stride pianists. It is equally easy to see how stride piano, with its strong echoes of ragtime, would seem retrogressive to Morton who had gone so far in stripping his playing of ragtime's characteristic right-hand figuration. (This might also explain why, in 1938, Morton singled out Bob Zurke as being "on the right track" for jazz piano: Zurke played an involved, melodic, emphatic non-ragtime style, one conceptually like Morton's but different in detail.) Thus Morton had a simpler, more modern, linear, and distinctly jazz-oriented right-hand style paired with an elaborate melodic bass style which, to other musicians, was reminiscent of ragtime. By contrast, stride had a strongly ragtime-influenced right-hand style dominated by figuration and a very clear, simpler, and more modern left-hand style.

In his left hand, Morton most often used the stridelike technique that he shared with ragtime and with the styles of many other jazz pianists well into the 1940s. Morton's version of this technique involves a great variety of first- and third-beat sonorities — single notes, fifths, sixths, sevenths, octaves, tenths, and triads — a frequent breaking out of a simple statement of the pulse into bass melodic figures, and a confining of the entire left-hand activity within a range of about two octaves and a half below, and a fifth above, middle C.

One effective way in which Morton and others used this left-hand technique was simply to break off from it, either not replacing it, in which case a break results, or using some other device, perhaps an active bass line in octaves. Morton used this latter device particularly effectively to enliven what might have been too regular a left-hand texture, or to reinforce important melodic features, or to mark phrase junctures.

When using the stridelike left-hand technique, Morton either could make the bass line formed by the lower notes of the first and third beats a traditional one emphasizing, most commonly, the root and fifth of the chord (as in *Grandpa's Spells,* [A¹-1], mm. 1 to 5), or he could use the lower register to shape a true linear part in counterpoint with the melody (as in *Grandpa's Spells,* [A¹-1], mm. 6 to 8).

A variation of the stridelike technique is the one used in, for instance, [C-1] of *Stratford Hunch.* Morton usually performed this left-hand style (which is rough-sounding because of the low-register placement of relatively small intervals) in such a way as to emphasize the line formed by the long notes played on the first and third beats, and played the afterbeats, by contrast, very short and sharply articulated.

The left-hand variations reflected Morton's belief that jazz piano must be orchestral in conception. Accordingly, the left hand could be purely rhythmic-harmonic in the commonest sort of stridelike use (most like a band's rhythm section), could play figures which recall New Orleans–style trombone or bass playing, or could become the lowest voice in a chordal segment.

(A left-hand usage fairly common in jazz piano but perhaps unfamiliar to some readers should be mentioned here because it produces music which, when examined out of context, can look or sound as if it contained mistakes. Sometimes a jazz pianist doubles the bass line with perfect fifths above [or, when octaves are played, perfect fifths above the lower pitches] irrespective of harmony. The intent, and the effect in a complete texture, is to make the doubled-bass line weightier.)

The variety of ways in which Morton used his right hand was also in keeping with his idea of orchestral style piano. This is true not only because of the particular devices he used (most of which are used by other jazz pianists as well), but because of the orderly way in which he used them to define, by their textural contrasts, choruses or parts of choruses. Sometimes he used his right hand to play sharply articulated chords, often widely spaced and dissonant, but overall his right-hand style was very linear; that is, it almost always projected singable melodic lines. Sometimes, as in parts of almost all of the "Spanish tinge" pieces, the melody becomes so independent that it appears to exist in a rhythmic framework different from that of the bass. At other times, as in [Cb-1] of *Perfect Rag,* the melodic line's repetitions, ornamental figuration, and speed create a texture that approximated that of eastern stride piano's post-ragtime style.

Morton played his principal melodic line either in single notes (alone or with harmony pitches above or below) or in octaves (with or without harmony pitches between). The harmony notes accompanying the melody have two functions more important than just increasing the right hand's density or supplying harmony (which in any case is explicitly stated by the left hand).

The first is rhythmic: the melody pitches which have the accompaniment of these harmony pitches are reinforced and accented, and the rhythm of this accentuation provides the main element of syncopation and rhythmic counterpoint to the left hand's relentlessly stated meter.

The second function of right-hand harmony pitches is that of controlling the smallest phrasing spans. Accompanied melody pitches initiate short spans of melody, that is, slurred phrases of two to five notes. Measure 6 of [a-2] of *New*

Orleans Blues contains a clear example of this: the effect of the D♭'s being slurred to C is created by the D♭'s G accompaniment. When Morton wishes to remove this effect, which depends upon the listener's hearing the accompanying note as if it were held through the phrase, he repeats the accompanying notes, creating a less legato, more emphatic effect, as in the corresponding place in the chorus before, [a-1].

(Readers should be aware that, when not playing the melody in octaves, Morton often placed his principal melodic line in the lower notes of his right hand, playing them more strongly than the notes above. Instances of this are not identified in the edition but they are usually obvious because the main melody is more active than the other lines and because its direction is so clear. For instance, in [B-1] of *Jelly Roll Blues* the melody is found in the lower, more active line in mm. 1, 2, and 5.)

Morton did not use much pedal. The overall legato quality of his playing, more obvious in the technically better, later recordings, was achieved almost entirely by the way he used his hands, holding down the keys for the maximum time possible before releasing them and moving his fingers to the new keys. The resulting ampleness of individual notes is responsible for the essential smoothness and unhurried rhythmic quality of his playing, even at fast tempos, and shows Morton's considerable control.

The steady quarter-note clicking in the Library of Congress recordings is Morton's foot on the pedal, a kind of tapping which he apparently did all of his life and which he and others have identified as his trademark. (It is also present, but less obvious, on some earlier recordings.) This tapping reveals an important aspect of Morton's conception of jazz meter: he thought in four beats per measure, in four-four time. Thus it is wrong, despite the two-beat flavor of some of his band records, particularly those of 1928 and 1929, to play Morton's music with too strongly emphasized first and third beats.

The reader will notice from the tempo indications given that Morton rushed in many performances. In most cases this is not easily noticeable. In others it is, particularly where there is not a steady increase in tempo. Fortunately, Morton does not seem to have had this trouble too often. (This unsteadiness obviously runs counter to the jazz ideal of a steady tempo, but a stopwatch will show that this ideal is seldom achieved: other jazz piano soloists — Johnson, Waller, Hines, Tatum — also rushed as much as Morton.)

The transcriptions here give a good survey of Morton's style: there are transcriptions of eleven performances from 1923 and 1924, a piano solo chorus from a band recording of 1926, two of the 1929 solos, twelve solos from the 1938 Library of Congress series, three others from Morton's Washington period, and three of the 1939 General solos.

The early performances were well planned and well played, and already show most of the range of Morton's composition and style which marked him as a unique pianist. In these, he plays his pieces rather formally for the most part, with little extended improvisation. (The contemporaneous piano rolls show that when Morton was not confined by the usual recording-time limit, he could and did improvise beautifully.) Conforming to the style of the period, Morton played swung* eighth notes with relatively long off-the-beat notes. As his 1934 recordings with Wingy Manone show, he continued to play this rhythmic style after others had turned to a more pronounced long-short division of the quarter-note pulse. (This is revealed only in Morton's solo chorus: in his ensemble playing and accompaniments for the other solos he follows the rhythmic style of the other players, showing that he knew and could play this newer style. He was responsible enough as an ensemble player not to try to impose his ideas on the other musicians.)

The 1929 Victor solos are not as well played as his other recordings, nor are his band recordings made later in the same week. The records sound as if they had been well planned — certainly the compositions are — but for some reason Morton's playing is somewhat inaccurate; he uses more pedal than usual (sometimes too much), rushes quite a bit, and loses his place once in each take of *Seattle Hunch,* even lapsing in one of them into *Frances* at the reappearance of the first strain. *Freakish* and *Pep,* both recorded at this time, are represented in this volume by transcriptions of their superior Library of Congress recordings.

The Library of Congress recordings are an extraordinary addition to the body of Morton recordings, and for that matter to the body of recorded jazz in general. Many of their faults, as well as their great beauties, stem from the fact that they were not well planned, commercially made recordings. Apparently Morton did not plan many of these performances, as evidence of occasional indecision seems to show, and he was apparently not in good health. (Whatever the making of these recordings meant to him, there was no reason for Morton to believe that they would ever be commercially available.)

On the other hand, these recordings captured Morton playing more extended, relaxed performances and show him to be an indefatigably inventive improvisor. On these recordings, not limited to just over three minutes as he was when making commercial, ten-inch, seventy-eight r.p.m. records, he performed more as he must have in person, going considerably beyond the more basic performances he recorded before and after. The recordings of *Kansas City Stomp, Jelly Roll Blues, Pep, Freakish,* and *Creepy Feeling* surpass his others; those of *Fickle Fay Creep, Jungle Blues, Sweet Peter,* and *Hyena Stomp* are excellent piano solo versions of pieces previously known only as band pieces; and the performances of *State and Madison, Bert Williams,* and *Spanish Swat* are Morton's only known recordings of these pieces, the latter two not even existing in notated form. (Some of this repertoire might seem a curious choice. Morton and Lomax spent some time reviewing the Library of Congress copyright deposit materials for the Morton pieces. On many of them, Lomax transcribed briefly Morton's comments on the pieces or on the notation, which in most cases was not by Morton. Many of these transcribed comments are dated June 6, 1938. Apparently Morton decided to play some of the pieces after reviewing the music, or simply when Lomax asked him to play them. Two performances, those of *Sweet Peter* and *State and Madison,* appear from their details to have been played from the copyright deposits themselves. The Library's reading room where Morton and Lomax examined the music is only a short distance from the building's Coolidge Auditorium where they recorded.)

The Library of Congress recordings show that by 1938 Morton had adopted the rhythmic style, with more pronounced long-short swung eighth-note differentiation, that he had been resisting in 1934.

Other changes on these recordings also indicate that Morton was setting a style which he was apparently not to change again. These changes were not great: they merely amplified or continued the evolution of certain features already part of his style and heard on earlier recordings. On his 1929 recordings Morton uses fewer left-hand octaves (on the first and third beats of measures) than he had used on earlier recordings, and the Library of Congress recordings continue this trend, showing more single notes and tenths instead. This is also a reflection of trends in jazz piano in general, which had been evolving away from the use of left-hand octaves since the earlier 1920s and, for that matter, even away from the stridelike left-hand style.

Morton's right-hand style also took on an added dimension. His earlier octave-dominated style was not abandoned, but now he often contrasted it with a lighter, more complicated style which hinted more strongly than ever at the presence of two melodic lines. His style had never before so nearly approximated the ensemble texture he saw as ideal for jazz piano.

Except for the privately recorded version of *The Pearls,* another lengthy performance, the remaining transcriptions are those of commercial recordings.

The four pieces from the 1939 General sessions, *Sporting House Rag, The Crave, Mr. Joe,* and *King Porter Stomp,* are well-planned performances of three-strain pieces played within the three-minute recording limit. They provide a good source for comparison with Morton's style of fifteen years earlier. His performances still present clearly the formal outlines of his compositions, but they are rhythmically looser, closer to the contemporary idea of swing, and they show a lighter filigree of embellishment and freer use of improvisation.

The direct influence of Morton's piano style was not great, perhaps because it was very personal and recognizable and because it was so tied to the performance of his own pieces. But when he arrived in Chicago, or anywhere except New York, Morton set standards for a level of technical accomplishment and complexity in solo piano which up to then had been represented only in New York, and then in a style much less oriented toward improvisation than his was.

The occasional claim that Morton was only a marginally competent pianist is completely refuted by the recordings: he was a remarkably strong pianist as many of his recordings (*Kansas City Stomp,* for instance) show. He was also an elegant pianist, as the Library of Congress recordings of *Creepy Feeling,* among others, demonstrates. Moreover, there is in Morton's playing a kind of overall virtuosity in his ability to establish and maintain a complete, active texture with striking independence of components — his band ideal — in which he has never been surpassed.

LIFE

THE LIFE

In spite of his lengthy recorded reminiscences, Jelly Roll Morton did not leave much precise biography. Only recently has Lawrence Gushee discovered, through imaginative research, the most basic facts of Morton's life, that he was born Ferdinand Joseph Lamothe, October 20, 1890.

Although Morton later explained that he had changed his name to avoid being called "Frenchy," the name Morton did not come out of the blue. Again from Gushee's research, we know that Morton's mother, Louise Monette, married William Mouton, later known as Morton, when Ferdinand was three years old.

Morton was a New Orleans Creole—of mixed black and European ancestry—a member of a group whose pride, pretensions, and prejudices, which he inherited, could be a source of strength. But these attitudes also caused hurt and isolation, as they did to Morton. During his childhood he was introduced to the still flourishing practice of voodoo by his godmother. Although he was raised a Roman Catholic, Morton early acquired a fear of voodoo which he apparently never lost.

His recorded recollections of his early life, as well as statements about his relatives, suggest that his great-grandmother and his aunt and uncle were in large measure responsible for raising him. His father was apparently absent from about 1902, and his mother died when he was about fifteen years old.

Morton also reminisced, in his Library of Congress interview with Alan Lomax, about a childhood in which music played a large part. He tells of experiences as a participant in New Orleans' legendary parades, as a member of the audience at the French Opera, and as a performer—guitarist, singer, trombonist, drummer, and sporting-house pianist. It is obvious that at an early age Morton was above all an attentive and impressionable listener. He appreciated and absorbed the beauties of all kinds of music, French and Italian opera—he later recalled specifically Verdi's *Il Trovatore* and Gounod's *Faust*—and other art music, the unsophisticated blues, the parade music, the gambling songs, the quadrilles and other dance music, the piano styles, the "Spanish" music, and the instrumental ragtime and jazz. In later years, when recalling for Lomax these sources of his own style, he could recreate them, treating them with respect and understanding even while identifying what he felt to be their respective weaknesses.

When Morton was about seventeen years old, his great-grandmother, wanting to remove his potentially bad influence on his two sisters, drove him from the house after learning that he worked as a sporting-house pianist. He thus began traveling at an early age, evidently never returning to New Orleans after about 1907.

He earned a living in a variety of ways: in addition to being a solo pianist and entertainer, he became a band leader, produced night club revues, managed night clubs, and became a vaudeville entertainer and musician. He seems too to have worked as a pimp and gambler. Until 1917, it was apparently Morton's practice to settle somewhere such as Mobile, Memphis, Chicago, or St. Louis for a short while and then to move on. For about five years, until May, 1923, his headquarters was in Los Angeles where he was involved in a variety of enterprises, including band-leading. This was apparently a very prosperous period for him during which he was in partnership with and lived with Anita Johnson Gonzales, whom he sometimes referred to as his wife (though it has not been established that they were legally married, and evidence suggests they were not). She figures in the titles of two of his pieces and was the author of the lyrics of *Dead Man Blues*.

In 1923, Morton returned to Chicago (for probably his third stay) without Anita and began his recording career and his association with the Melrose Brothers Music Company (see the introductory essay for *Wolverine Blues*). Walter and Lester Melrose published solo piano and dance- or jazz-band versions of Morton's pieces, issuing them after Morton had recorded them. Undoubtedly the brothers helped in securing the recording contracts for OKeh, Gennett, Paramount, and still-smaller labels. In September, 1926, Morton began to record for Victor. His 1926 and 1927 Victor records apparently sold very well: Victor billed Morton's Red Hot Peppers as their best-selling "hot" band. Melrose continued to issue single-copy and folio editions of his piano music, sheet-music editions of the vocal pieces, and orchestrations based on the records. In 1929 the Melrose brothers issued their last orchestration of a Morton piece, *Georgia Swing*, based, as were all of them after 1926, on the Morton recording. The Melrose advertising at that time listed eighty-two orchestrations, twenty-three of these arrangements of Morton compositions and eight of them pieces which Morton had recorded but did not compose.

Early in 1928, at the peak of his success, Morton moved to New York. He had become increasingly aware of the business, as well as the performance, aspects of jazz, and New York was now the center of its growing business activity — booking, publishing, recording, and broadcasting.

In November, 1928, on a return visit to the Midwest, Morton married Mabel Bertrand, a New Orleans Creole whom he had met before moving to New York while she was working as a show girl in Chicago.

Morton's recordings after his arrival in New York apparently achieved neither the considerable commercial success, nor often the artistic success, of his Chicago records. He tried the big-band idiom on recordings, having already used for some time a ten-piece group (that period's version of a big band) as his working group. Although he was more than a routinely competent arranger, his stylistic frame of reference at this time was, or seemed to be, dated: he either had not learned the lessons of the New York musicians' emerging big-band style and rhythmic concepts, or he chose, for the sake of his own principles, simply not to adopt them. Apparently only too willing to point out to New York musicians the mistakes in their notions about jazz and to insist on strict deportment for sidemen, he earned a reputation as a difficult leader. He was hampered by unstable, relatively undistinguished personnel, and probably an inability to discipline his groups adequately in order to meet an ever-rising standard of ensemble playing. As a result, his 1928 and 1929 ten- and eleven-piece recording groups produced music more like that of the contemporaneous (and already somewhat dated)

Bennie Moten band of Kansas City, rather than that of such innovative or mainstream New York groups as Duke Ellington's, Fletcher Henderson's, Luis Russell's, or Charlie Johnson's, the groups with which he was competing.

Morton had a highly developed sense of principle and knew exactly what his music meant and how it was to work. At that time, his musical ideas were better realized by small groups, and in late 1929 when he returned to recording with groups of seven or eight pieces that were not so dependent upon the section concept the results were generally more musically successful and rhythmically nearer the stylistic mainstream than his work with larger ensembles. Nevertheless, smaller, freer groups ran counter to the prevailing trends, and his Victor contract, when it expired in 1930, was not renewed (though recordings he had made until that time continued to be released until 1933).

The early and middle 1930s were difficult for Morton, as well as for all jazz musicians. Because of his inability or unwillingness to keep up with contemporary styles, Morton was now unable to keep a band working consistently, and he had to make his living as a soloist, sideman, or accompanist. Morton also had business troubles unrelated to music, and in addition spent a substantial amount of money going to a voodoo practitioner trying to remove a voodoo curse.

Most of the stories of Morton's abrasive personality and monumental self-esteem date from this period (1930 to 1935) of dwindling success and prestige. When on the defensive, as was now often the case, Morton seemed a big-talking has-been. (It has been my observation that musicians who knew Morton in Chicago had more respect and affection for him than those who only knew him superficially in New York.)

Morton's days as a band leader on records were temporarily over. Between his last Victor session in 1930 and the Library of Congress recordings in 1938, he is known to have had only one recording session. This was as a sideman in a 1934 Wingy Manone session in New York, in which he played a beautiful, if somewhat anachronistic, solo. Through the 1930s, several of his previously published compositions, particularly *King Porter Stomp* and *Milenberg Joys*, were occasionally recorded by Fletcher Henderson, the Dorsey brothers, the Casa Loma Orchestra, Bennie Moten, Bob Crosby, Harry James, Glen Miller, Bennie Goodman, and a few others. But no new music of his was published until 1938.

In 1936 Morton went to Washington, D.C., without Mabel, to become a prize-fight promoter, but he soon began managing and playing in what is reported to have been a very sleazy night club, known at various times as The Music Box, The Blue Moon Inn, and the Jungle Club. Mabel joined him in 1937. In 1938 Morton was attacked in his club and wounded in the head and chest. This incident aggravated his health problems, which sometimes incapacitated him during the rest of his life. Two important events date from these Washington days: Morton's five-week recording session of music and talking, recorded by Alan Lomax in the Library of Congress' Coolidge Auditorium, and his association with Roy Carew, who attempted to be of practical help by publishing some of his music.

In December, 1938, partly at Mabel's urging, he left the night club, even though he was still optimistic about its success, and returned with her to New York. He hoped to revive his career and had reason for hope: starting with his famous letter to Robert Ripley and *Downbeat* magazine—meant to set straight the record about his and W. C. Handy's relative importance in jazz history — and with publicity resulting from the Library of Congress recording sessions, Morton again became the object of some interest, though perhaps more as a historic figure than as the vital musician he still was. He appeared on two nationwide radio broadcasts, Gabriel Heatter's "We, The People," in October, 1939, and NBC's "Chamber Music Society of Lower Basin Street," in July, 1940.

He made a few of his finest solo recordings and some beautiful piano-vocal ones at this time, including *The Crave* and *King Porter Stomp* (transcribed in this volume) and *Mamie's Blues* and *Winin' Boy Blues*. There were also some less successful band recordings and the reissue of several of his earlier Victor records. But prevailing tastes in jazz were neither ready for the traditional jazz revival, which was to benefit many of his colleagues only a few years later, nor willing to accept his still-unchanged style as other than a historical survival. This, coupled with his failing health (he suffered from asthma and a heart condition for which he was hospitalized for three months) permitted him only modest success, and he was forced to accept a small weekly check from Catholic Charities.

In November, 1940, driving his Lincoln and towing his Cadillac, Morton went to Los Angeles in order to protect the interests of his recently widowed blind godfather and to benefit from a climate more favorable to his health. Little is known of his activities in California, but he wrote to Roy Carew of a projected appearance on Orson Welles's radio program, and he renewed his association with Anita. His letters to Mabel tell of increasingly incapacitating illness. He entered Los Angeles County General Hospital and died there in Anita's arms eleven days later on July 10, 1941, of heart failure resulting from chronic high blood pressure. His peculiar will, dated June 28, 1941, and apparently prepared by someone else for his signature, did not even mention Mabel. Except for Morton's interest in Carew's publications, which was bequeathed to his sister Amède Colas, the will left everything of value, including royalties from Melrose, Southern Music Company, and ASCAP, to Anita.

From about 1930 Morton seems to have been victimized by his own prejudices and phobias, his tardy adjustment to prevailing realities, missed opportunities, and bad luck, especially in his inability to organize and keep steadily working a band with stable personnel. (Regular work with stable personnel was the basis of the success of many groups, even when they did not have star performers.)

Another important problem was the hold voodoo evidently had on Morton. According to Mabel, as well as himself, his efforts to rid himself of its influence were responsible for the loss of much of his prosperity in the early 1930s.

Being a New Orleans Creole was a source of pride and strength for Morton; it was the cornerstone of his musical and personal makeup. In an earlier age and in another place, such qualities might have made him an aristocrat. But they were meaningless in the northern black world of the 1930s, except perhaps in a negative way, because they formed the basis for attitudes which estranged Morton from many other musicians, some of whom found him arrogant. And his insistence on his own way of playing probably seemed to them less a matter of principle than the action of a dated musician unable to keep up. Morton seems, of necessity, eventually to have overcome some of the musical problems which restrained his success, but he did so too late.

Several of Morton's later recordings, in addition to continuing his proven earlier style, point to new, promising directions that he might have taken. But Morton died before they could be realized and before he could benefit from the changing attitudes toward jazz and jazz musicians which materially and spiritually helped so substantially those who survived him. When he died, not yet fifty-one years old, only a part of the jazz community took note.

During his lifetime, the intrinsic merit of Morton's work was not recognized. Among some, he may still be unappreciated. However, now at last his true value as a remarkable, unique composer and pianist, a musician who ranks among the very finest jazz has produced and who made important contributions to that genre, is becoming known.

CHRONOLOGY OF COMPOSITIONS

CHRONOLOGY OF COMPOSITIONS

A chronology of the actual composition of the pieces in this volume is impossible to establish with certainty. Although dates of first recordings and copyrights for the pieces are easy to establish through current discographical reference works and copyright records, less reliable data, such as Morton's statements and those of others, and speculations based upon known conjunctions of time and place, can be used only with caution to establish chronology.

The chronology for the pieces in the volume, listed below, is as accurate as the data will allow. Material within brackets comes from recollections of musicians, hearsay, and historical reconstruction and cannot be substantiated. Material not in brackets lists the first documented evidence, a copyright or recording, of the existence of a composition, but many of them had probably been composed years earlier. Additional historical information for many of the pieces may be found in the introductory essay to the music.

[1902: *New Orleans Blues* composed in this year, according to Morton's recorded conversation with Lomax. But according to Morton's letter to Ripley and *Downbeat,* the year of composition was 1905.]

[1905: *Jelly Roll Blues* composed in this year, according to Roy Carew and Morton's letter to Ripley. James P. Johnson recalled having heard Morton play it in New York in 1911.]

[1906: *King Porter Stomp* composed, according to Carew.]

[1908: *Frog-I-More Rag* composed, according to Carew.]

[ca. 1910-1911: *The Crave* composed (?). See introductory essay for the piece.]

[1911 or earlier: *Bert Williams* composed. See introductory essay.]

[ca. 1915-1916: *Wolverine Blues* composed in Detroit, according to Morton.]

September 15, 1915: *Jelly Roll Blues* copyrighted by Will Rossiter, Chicago. (See entry for 1905.)

May 15, 1918: *Frog-I-More Rag* copyrighted by Ferd Morton, Los Angeles. (See entry for 1908.)

[1919: *Kansas City Stomp* and *The Pearls* composed, according to Morton.]

February 14, 1923: *Wolverine Blues* copyrighted, as by Spikes, Morton, Spikes, by the Melrose Brothers Music Company, Chicago. (See entry for 1915-1916.)

June, 1923: *Big Foot Ham* first recorded, by Jelly Roll Morton and his Orchestra. This was Morton's first known recording session.

July 17, 1923: *King Porter Stomp* (see entry for 1906) and *New Orleans Blues* (see entry for 1902) first recorded, as piano solos. *Mr. Jelly Lord* first recorded, by the New Orleans Rhythm Kings with Morton at the piano.

July 18, 1923: *Grandpa's Spells, Kansas City Stomp* (see entry for 1919), and *The Pearls* (see entry for 1919) first recorded, as piano solos. *London Blues* first recorded, by the New Orleans Rhythm Kings with Morton at the piano.

ca. April, 1924: *Mamanita* first recorded, as a piano solo. The title suggests that the piece might date from Morton's California days with Anita Gonzalez.

June 9, 1924: *Shreveport Stomp, Perfect Rag* (retitled *Sporting House Rag* in 1939), *Tom Cat Blues,* and *Stratford Hunch* first recorded, as piano solos.

September 25, 1925: *Queen of Spades* copyrighted, in an orchestration, by Melrose. Within a year the piece was retitled *Black Bottom Stomp.*

May 12, 1926: *Soap Suds* recorded by the St. Louis Levee Band, perhaps a small group drawn from Morton's touring group of the time, with Morton at the piano. The piece was later (1930) retitled *Fickle Fay Creep.*

July 3, 1926: *Dead Man Blues,* with lyrics by Anita Gonzalez, copyrighted by Melrose. Anita's authorship of the lyrics suggests that the piece might have been composed three to nine years earlier. Morton's QRS roll also dates from this year, perhaps even from before the copyright.

August 7, 1926: *State and Madison* copyrighted by Charles Raymond, Chicago, one of two co-composers.

December 10, 1926: *Cannonball Blues* copyrighted by Melrose.

February 5, 1927: *Ted Lewis Blues,* about ten weeks later to be retitled *Wild Man Blues,* copyrighted by Melrose.

June 4, 1927: *Hyena Stomp, Billy Goat Stomp,* and *Jungle Blues* first recorded, by the Red Hot Peppers, Morton's recording group.

March 13, 1928: *Buffalo Blues* first recorded, by Johnny Dunn and his band with Morton at the piano. Morton later recorded the piece, solo, as *Mr. Joe,* which may have been the original title. See the introductory essay for this piece. According to Charles Edward Smith, the piece dates from Morton's New Orleans days, that is, 1907 or earlier, and it was played by King Oliver's Creole Jazz Band, which would mean that it had been heard as early as 1923.

June 11, 1928: *Georgia Swing* and *Boogaboo* first recorded, by the Red Hot Peppers. Later, in his letter to Ripley, Morton maintains, in the course of claiming the first use of the word "swing" applied to jazz, that *Georgia Swing* had been written in 1907.

July 8, 1929: *Pep, Seattle Hunch, Frances,* and *Freakish* first recorded, as piano solos. *Pep* and *Freakish* probably were composed at about this time, since they both appear to be what might be thought of as "up-to-date" pieces. *Frances* strongly resembles the earlier *Mamanita.*

November 13, 1929: *Sweet Peter* first recorded, by the Red Hot Peppers.

November 18, 1930: *Dixie Knows* copyrighted, in an orchestration, by Melrose.

May-June, 1938: *Bert Williams* (see entry for 1911), *Creepy Feeling, Spanish Swat,* and *The Crave* (see entry for 1910-1911) first recorded, as piano solos, during the Library of Congress sessions.

December, 1938: *Fingerbuster* and *Honky Tonk Music* first recorded, as piano solos. *Fingerbuster* was at least a few months older than this, since Morton had mentioned it months before to Lomax. But it is probably much older than this. See the introductory essay for this piece.

NOTES
ON THE MUSIC AND EDITORIAL PROCEDURES

NOTES ON THE MUSIC AND EDITORIAL PROCEDURES

The forty pieces in this volume can be divided into four categories according to their sources: (1) editions of music originally published for piano solo; (2) editions of music originally published for piano solo but based upon recorded ensemble versions; (3) transcriptions of piano rolls; and (4) transcriptions of recorded piano performances. The latter constitute by far the largest group. Insofar as is possible, the order of the pieces is chronological, according to date of recording or date of copyright. Thus the pieces, taken in order, show the changes in Morton's style from 1923 to 1939. A chronology of the compositions themselves, as opposed to the performances, is given beginning on page 23.

As far as we know, the first printed piano-solo version of one of Morton's pieces was the 1915 Will Rossiter publication of *Jelly Roll Blues.* This was followed, beginning in 1923, by the Melrose brothers' publication of ten piano-solo versions of Morton pieces, *Wolverine Blues, Kansas City Stomp, Grandpa's Spells, London Blues, New Orleans Blues, The Pearls, Chicago Breakdown, King Porter Stomp, Shreveport Stomp,* and *Deuces Wild.* (The last piece was advertised but was never copyrighted and has not been found. Its title suggests that it may be the piece which first appeared as *Queen of Spades* and was then retitled *Black Bottom Stomp.*) Of these, *Kansas City Stomp, Grandpa's Spells, London Blues,* and *The Pearls* are almost identical in their published forms to the copyright deposit versions at the Library of Congress in Morton's own hand. This suggests that they were prepared for publication from his own notated versions. The others of this group have a very similar notational style and are, as well, the nearest of any published versions to Morton's actual recorded performances. The Melrose first folio, apparently initially published in 1927, collected all of these separately published pieces, in addition to *Dead Man Blues* and *Jelly Roll Blues.* Single-copy versions of later pieces, and the two additional folios collecting them, did not faithfully represent Morton's playing style.

All music edited from printed sources has had measure numbers and formal designations of sections added. *Black Bottom Stomp,* never recorded as a solo, has had dynamics and articulation markings added. The extent of other editorial changes, in order to make the printed version conform more closely to Morton's style, may be seen from examples given with the music. *Dixie Knows,* apparently never recorded by Morton in any medium, is reprinted as originally published.

The five piano-solo versions of pieces from band recordings are *Cannonball Blues, Billy Goat Stomp, Wild Man Blues, Georgia Swing,* and *Boogaboo.* Except for *Cannonball Blues,* which seems to have been published before it was recorded, they were probably issued to take advantage of the fact that there were Morton Red Hot Peppers recordings of the pieces then available. As a group, they were somewhat less successfully notated for piano than the others, not only because of the changed medium and their essentially small scale, but also because the arrangers who prepared them did not have Morton's skill in constructing variations. (Morton himself showed, with his later versions of *Hyena Stomp* and *Jungle Blues,* that pieces first recorded by eight instruments could make effective piano solos.) These versions are rather short—since faithful transcriptions of the band performances for piano are not feasible—and usually state only the basic material. Except for *Cannonball Blues,* each of these pieces has only two strains.

Cannonball Blues, already cast in a style closer to Morton's than that of the other piano-into-band versions, has been edited to make it conform better to Morton's piano style and to reflect the formal recasting of his band version. *Billy Goat Stomp* is reprinted as originally published and is included mainly for the sake of completeness, since it does not survive so well in its change of medium from band to piano. The edition of *Wild Man Blues* adds only dynamic and articulation markings and some corrected misspellings of the original. *Georgia Swing* and *Boogaboo* make attractive, if brief, piano solos. In *Georgia Swing*'s edition some mistakes in the melody line are corrected and dynamic and articulation markings have been added. It closes with a piano reduction of the last chorus of the Red Hot Peppers recording of the piece. *Boogaboo*'s dynamic and articulation markings are added, some misspellings are corrected and some uncharacteristic "modernisms" are removed from the harmony. For each of these pieces, examples of the editorial changes made are given in notes following the complete version of the piece.

Mr. Jelly Lord and *Dead Man Blues* are each represented principally by their piano-roll performances. Each was performed on a "word roll," one with the piece's lyrics printed at the side of the perforations for those who wished to sing along. A word roll had to state the melody rather explicitly and this imposed limits on the performance as a vehicle for jazz improvisation. Nevertheless, Morton dealt with these limitations quite successfully and, particularly in the case of *Mr. Jelly Lord,* produced rolls of considerable interest.

Piano rolls are uniquely susceptible of alteration before publication: notes can be added or removed simply by adding or filling in holes in the master roll. Each of these rolls bears aural evidence of having been altered; indeed some of the passages are impossible for a solo player. I have removed obvious stylistic anomalies and have indicated in the notes following the pieces what the rolls actually play. I have not removed the more subtle differences between the style of these rolls and that of the recorded performances. These are differences which probably are the result of editorial change but which might have been introduced by Morton himself. With a little information on the differences, the reader can remove them himself (if he assumes that these changes were added editorially) or he can play the transcriptions in order to produce the music as it is on the rolls.

There are two principal differences between the performances on the rolls and Morton's style on his recordings. First, the rolls often seem to include more harmony notes between the notes of the octave playing the melody, which gives a somewhat less bright, less incisive right-hand style. Second, the left hand often contains sustained middle-register notes—usually within a fifth below middle C—introduced as the top notes of octaves or tenths.

While Morton possibly could have introduced the change in his right-hand style, especially if he made the rolls at a slow tempo, I think it more likely that the extra notes were added by an editor. The reader can thin the right-hand texture by removing notes, keeping (usually) the thirds or sevenths of chords, and the notes preceded by accidentals.

Transcription of the rolls' left-hand style sometimes produces music that cannot actually be played. Long notes—appearing as the tops of octaves and tenths on beats one and three—are often held for two to four beats. With the use of the pedal and a rethinking of the left-hand technique, an approximation of this effect, a sound common in popular music piano playing of the 1920s and 1930s, can be produced. I have transcribed the roll's left hand as much as possible as the roll actually plays, even while questioning the authenticity of this style. The reader can adopt the style or discard it—simply by cutting short these long notes—as he sees fit.

(Biograph BLP 1004Q is an LP recording of all of Morton's known rolls. Some of the long left-hand notes are missing in these recordings because Michael Montgomery, who edited the rolls, judiciously removed them. Montgomery is a piano-roll collector and expert as well as a pianist.)

One further difference between the style of the rolls and that of the recordings is in the use of repetition of large segments of music. Literal repetition of a section is possible through the duplication of the appropriate sequence of holes in the piano roll. Each of the performances transcribed fully here makes some use of repetition of whole choruses, which accounts for the use of repeat signs in these transcriptions.

The remaining thirty-one compositions are transcribed from recorded performances, beginning with Morton's first solo recording session for Gennett in 1923, and ending with his last solo recording session in 1939. The principle I have used for these transcriptions is to notate just what Morton played. My exceptions were: (1) mistakes which seem obvious (for these I have notated what I believe Morton intended and have indicated in a note the mistake he actually played); (2) places in which I cannot be certain what Morton played, for which I have provided a conjectural solution and so identified it; (3) "rips," the two-, three-, or four-note ascending scalewise ornaments rising to a principal melody pitch, which I have often notated as successions of grace notes, in spite of slight rhythmic differences; and (4) some of the middle-register second- and fourth-beat left-hand chords whose highest pitch is usually audible, but whose precise spacing below and sometimes even pitch content are unclear. For these chords I have notated what I know Morton played in other, more audible, instances when he used the same harmony. Such notations are not identified as conjectural.

The main difficulty in transcribing piano music is that of register: not whether any C's are being played, but which ones are being played. This arises from the nature of the piano itself, and especially from the large pianos usually found in recording studios, which have rich spectra of overtones. Two rather different problems emerge. The first problem is that the harmonics generated by lower notes are occasionally strong enough—particularly the twelfth above the fundamental—to sound as if they had actually been played. This is especially prevalent on acoustical recordings.

The second problem is the opposite one: notes that actually were played can get lost, particularly when they are very high. Relatively weak upper octave doublings of strongly played lower notes (which describes the way Morton played right-hand octaves) are somewhat fainter and "hide" in the upper partials of the lower pitches. (Some aspects of Morton's playing suggest that he conceived of the lower pitch of a right-hand octave as the principal one.)

The notation in this volume is meant not only to be an accurate recording of what Morton played, but also to be uncomplicated enough to be playable. Thus notations could sometimes have been made still more rhythmically precise. But every gain in such accuracy calls for another musical symbol, and the notation would then become progressively more complicated and less useful as it begins to bristle with refinements. Nevertheless, the relatively uncomplicated notation in this volume, given the assumptions explained below, is quite accurate, and the recordings themselves can answer questions about further refinements.

In many cases, details of articulation or very small distinctions in rhythm are not reflected in the notation. For instance the stridelike left hand, almost always notated here with four quarter-note durations, is often played with the second- and fourth-beat chords played short and sharply articulated, suggesting a notation of [musical notation]. I have not used distinctions of this magnitude because I wished to avoid complexity and, more importantly, because I wished to show important similarities rather than what I think are fairly unimportant differences.

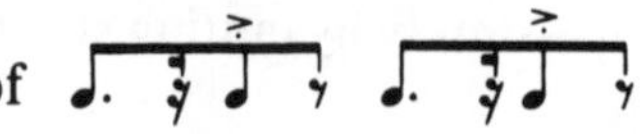

The notation of jazz raises the question of just what notation can actually represent. It should be borne in mind that modern music notation developed largely as a prescriptive system, designed to give performers directions on how to realize a piece in performance. In this volume it is being used descriptively, to record performances that have already taken place.

Our notational system, with a simple proportional scheme for rhythm, does not lend itself to descriptive use for jazz because rhythms that the system cannot easily record are commonplace. (A truly accurate notation of a performance—as opposed to the composition itself—of a Western classical piece with its rubato would be similarly difficult to achieve.) An explanation, then, of the assumptions made in my use of notation is necessary.

No truly satisfactorily simple or universally used system for the notation of jazz's swung "eighth" notes exists. The general principle of this jazz convention is that two notes played consecutively during a quarter-note beat will not be equal in duration: the first will be longer, producing the characteristic long-short rhythmic feel of jazz. While jazz practice from time to time reestablishes norms of what is acceptable in what tempo as the proportional relationship of these two durations, the proportions are generally governed by the following limits: the faster the tempo is, the more nearly equal the "eighth" notes are; and the slower the tempo is, the more nearly the proportion approaches being [musical notation]. In this volume and in much jazz notation elsewhere, ordinary undifferentiated eighth notes are used to represent the swung eighth-note rhythm. Almost all of the eighth notes in this volume are to be played swung, as are all syncopations. (These latter might be thought of as tied eighth notes; e.g., [musical notation] can be thought of as [musical notation].) The relatively rare evenly played eighth notes are identified by horizontal dashes, enclosed within parentheses, above or below the noteheads, e.g. [musical notation] or [musical notation]. In the "Spanish tinge"* pieces or sections of pieces, *New Orleans Blues, Mamanita, Dead Man Blues, Creepy Feeling, Spanish Swat, Honky Tonk Music,* and *The Crave,* the eighth notes are swung, but are generally more nearly equal in duration. The left-hand tango or habañera rhythm, which is syncopated, is also swung.

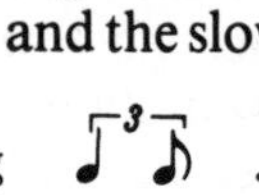

As I have done with the notation of the stridelike left hand, I have used a shortcut in the notation of the left hand of the "Spanish tinge" pieces and sections of pieces: the left-hand rhythm's commonest form is notated ♩. ♪♩ ♩ for the sake of simplicity, though Morton often actually plays this as ♪. 𝄿𝄾♪𝄽 ♪𝄾 .

In general, the "Spanish tinge" pieces present the greatest rhythmic difficulties. Here again, more discriminant notation could have been used (indeed my working transcriptions were more complicated than the notations in this volume), but I have chosen to represent difficult passages as simply as possible. In the notes following the pieces I have identified the few segments in which notes of very slightly different lengths are represented as being equal in time value.

Ghost notes* in the transcriptions are enclosed within parentheses.

At several points in the music there are indications for simultaneous grace notes. These are attacked with, not before, the principal notes but are released immediately while the principal notes are held.

The only other unconventional notation that I have used is the adding of a stem to the notehead of a note which, as indicated by the stem, is actually held slightly beyond its duration as represented by the conventional part of the notation. Thus such a segment as  represents four eighth notes with the second held slightly longer than the others, a little beyond the attack of the note which follows.

A few small problems make absolutely precise determination of tempo difficult or impossible. Although it is known in what key most of the pieces were played, a crucial point with the Library of Congress recordings, which were recorded on equipment that in some cases slowed them down enough to lower the pitch almost a minor third, there cannot be absolute certainty about the pitch to which the pianos were tuned. The tempo indications, which are corrected to the proper pitch as nearly as possible, should nevertheless be accurate within very few beats. For the performances which rush, I have given the average tempo for the first and last whole choruses*. The tempo indications for the reprinted sheet music and the piano-roll transcriptions are those of other performances of the same or similar pieces.

The designation of strains* also needs explanation. Since the effect of immediate repetition of a strain is not the same as the effect of its reappearance after other material has intervened, I have used symbols which recognize this difference in designating the strains. The representation A^1-1; A^1-2; B^1-1; B^1-2; A^2; B^2-1; B^2-2 can be read as: first strain/group one–first appearance; first strain/group one–second appearance; second strain/group one–first appearance; second strain/group one–second appearance; first strain/group two (one appearance only); second strain/second group–first appearance; second strain/second group–second appearance. Where I have used lower-case letters, in the blues pieces for instance, the strains are identical in length, very similar in harmonic outline, and distinguished by only relatively small melodic and textural differences.

The introductory essays give outlines of the pieces' copyright histories, showing the dates of copyright, the forms in which the pieces were copyrighted (i.e., lead sheet, piano solo version, orchestration), and the original copyright holders. They also give histories of Morton recordings of the pieces, showing dates of recording, artists and/or media, record label and issue numbers with master numbers in parentheses, and metronomic tempo indications, which show ranges of tempos within which Morton played the pieces.

Following each introductory essay is the music itself, a complete version of the piece (followed, in several cases, by additional notations which transcribe parts of other performances to show how Morton played the same material differently at different times) with notes on the transcription or edition at the end.

The source which is transcribed in its entirety, either a recording or printed music, is identified in the copyright and recording history with an asterisk. The source of any additional partial notation is identified with a +.

At the end of the volume is a glossary of terms used in the text.

Discographical information is from Brian Rust's *Jazz Records, 1897–1942.*

Finally, the reader should be aware that these are not the "correct" or "definitive" versions of Morton's pieces: indeed there cannot be such versions of pieces into which variability is composed. Rather, the complete versions transcribed are those in which I thought Morton the performer and Morton the composer were best balanced and in which the piece as a whole was best realized.

WOLVERINE BLUES

MICHIGAN

A.U. BROWN

Successfully Introduced by the New Orleans Rythm Kings

WORDS & MUSIC BY

BENJAMIN SPIKES · FERD MORTON & JOHN SPIKES

PRINTED IN THE U.S.A.

"FULL OF ORIGINALITY"

THE "JELLY ROLL" BLUES

(FOX-TROT)

BY

FERD MORTON

AUTHOR OF "THE "JELLY ROLL" BLUES" SONG

5

Published for BAND and ORCHESTRA

WILL ROSSITER
THE CHICAGO PUBLISHER
136 W. LAKE ST. CHICAGO, ILL.

KING PORTER STOMP
"Jelly Roll" Morton's
famous
Blues & Rag Series
WOLVERINE BLUES
KANSAS CITY STOMPS
GRANDPA'S SPELLS
LONDON BLUES
NEW ORLEANS BLUES
THE PEARLS
CHICAGO BREAKDOWN
DEUCES WILD
KING PORTER
SHREVEPORT STOMPS
Price 60 Cents
MELROSE BROS.
MUSIC COMPANY
CHICAGO, ILL.

FOLIO NO.1

"JELLY ROLL" MORTON'S

FAMOUS SERIES OF

Blues & Stomps

FOR PIANO

"Jelly Roll" Morton
Exclusive Victor Artist

The following Selections are his most Famous Compositions

Contents

Wolverine Blues,
King Porter Stomp
New Orleans Blues
Black Bottom Stomp
London Blues
Chicago Breakdown
The Pearls
Kansas City Stomp
Grandpa's Spells
Dead Man Blues
Shreeveport Stomp
The Original "Jelly Roll" Morton Blues

PRICE 50¢

MADE IN U.S.A.

THE MUSIC

NEW ORLEANS BLUES
also known as NEW ORLEANS JOYS

COPYRIGHT:

April 1, 1925: orchestration, Melrose Brothers Music Company.

RECORDINGS:

(*)July 17, 1923 (as *New Orleans Joys*): piano solo; Gennett 5486 (*11538, 11538-A); ♩ = c. 136,
May 21-July, 1938: piano solo, recorded (1681) in the Library of Congress by Alan Lomax; ♩ = c. 122 increasing to c. 125.

Morton identified *New Orleans Blues* as one of his earliest compositions. The work is a blues* in a graceful "Spanish tinge"* style, simple, impressively controlled, and highlighted in this performance by a climactic rhythmically intricate chorus. The solidity of the final chorus closes the piece effectively. Morton was justifiably proud of this early piece and was careful, when telling Alan Lomax about it, to identify Frank Richards, a teacher of his, as having been helpful in its composition. He spoke of the work as one of the first blues* as a playable composition; that is, it turned one of jazz's most durable structures, the twelve-measure blues, from a mere harmonic pattern for improvisation into a composition with predetermined melodies, textures, and order of elements.

The five-measure introduction is unusual but makes perfectly good sense. The first three measures define the tonality and, with their octaves and parallel movements, are obviously introductory. When this opening flourish cadences on the first beat of the fourth measure, the tango-rhythm left hand appears and, as in a vamp*, is heard for two measures before the melody begins, establishing this left-hand procedure in the listener's mind. (An interesting experiment is to play the introduction without the fifth measure, shortening it to the more regular four measures: the melody seems then to enter too soon.)

Morton's system of interior repetitions was effectively developed in this piece, and in a rather subtle way. Note first that the most variable element in the chorus is the first four-measure segment. Next, notice what is repeated from chorus to chorus: measures 5, 6, 7, 8, 9, and 10 of [a-1] are repeated almost literally in [a-2]; only measures 5, 6, and 7 are repeated in [b-1]; only measures 5 and 6 in [b-2]; only 6 in [c-1]. Finally, with [c-2][1] the repetitions are eliminated altogether with Morton's startlingly complicated improvising. (Some currently available reissues of this recording, apparently edited after dubbing to tape by removing a span of tape, make it sound as if Morton's timing falters near the beginning of [c-2]. It did not, as a playing of the unaltered original illustrates. It would have been much better to let stand a pop or hiss than to distort a performance in this way.) With the interior repetitions now pared down literally to nothing, Morton's beautiful last chorus, labeled "stomp" in the original publication and breaking into the stridelike left hand for the first time in the piece, appears and alludes to the interior repetitions again in measures 5, 6, 7, and 8, restoring in varied form this segment of repeated music.

The second take, apparently recorded immediately after this one, is more rhythmically complicated than this one, but spreads the complexity over a longer time span, weakening its effectiveness somewhat, and does not so clearly carry out the system of interior repetitions (which also appears in the published version of the piece).

[1]This is called [c-2] here in spite of only slight similarity to [c-1] because it is obvious from the second take that Morton conceived of the first six choruses as presenting three variations, each immediately repeated.

New Orleans Blues

* Simultaneous grace note

[a-2]
mf

[b-1]
mf
(1)
(2)
dim.
p
cresc.
mf
[b-2]

* Simultaneous grace note.

[c-2]
(5)
mf
5:4
7:6
6:5
3:2

cresc.
f
[d]
f

1. On each of his three recordings of this piece Morton played the first four notes of this figure —and their repetitions—differently. On the second Gennett take, he substitutes G for the A♭. On the Library of Congress recording the first four notes of the figure are B♭, A♭, G, and F.
2. An F rather than G actually sounds in this chord.
3. Morton also plays faintly an E♮ below the top F.
4. With the G and C Morton restrikes the F he had just left.
5. Like the notation of similarly difficult segments of "Spanish tinge" pieces in the volume, the notation of this chorus, despite a basic rightness, conveys little of the subtlety of Morton's playing, not even attempting to show minute variations of time value. The first, third, and fourth measures' eighth notes are not equal in duration, nor are they all attacked precisely where the notation places them. Here, as in other such pieces, the recording must be consulted.

GRANDPA'S SPELLS

COPYRIGHT:

August 20, 1923: piano solo version, Morton holograph; Melrose Brothers Music Company,
April 1, 1925: orchestration; Melrose Brothers Music Company.

RECORDINGS:

*July 18, 1923: piano solo; Gennett 5218 (11544); ♩ = c. 210 increasing to 216,
+ 1924: piano roll; Vocalstyle 50487,
(+)December 16, 1926: Jelly Roll Morton's Red Hot Peppers; + Bluebird B-10254 (37255-2), Victor 20431 (37255-3); ♩ = c. 193.

Grandpa's Spells, an attractive three-strain piece, does not appear in Morton's work until 1923. It was probably written earlier, perhaps much earlier, as two things suggest. First, Morton's own holograph of the piece, of which the Melrose publication is an almost exact printing, is Morton's only holograph notation in the Library of Congress in two-four time, ragtime's common meter signature. Second, Morton's performance of the first strain* has more in common with ragtime than any of his other early recordings, including even *Perfect Rag,* further suggesting an early origin.

The first strain has a rather naive melody for Morton, one which he apparently thought little enough of by 1926 to gloss over on his band recording. He makes the best possible use of this strain on his solo recording and on his piano roll by improvising fine choruses on it.

The other two strains rank with Morton's best: the second, a beautiful one with its counterpoint of melody and bass line; and the third, rather rifflike*, another Morton forecast of the kind of structure which other jazzmen would later find to be such a good basis for improvisation.

An interesting Morton style feature is the left hand in measures 2, 4, 10, and 12 of [C-1] and [C-2] which seems to turn the beat around by exchanging the normal positions of weak- and strong-beat events. Morton used this on other recordings, too, notably on the Gennett *Kansas City Stomp,* on which he maintained it, uninterrupted, for six full measures in a reprise of the first strain, and in the band version of *Wild Man Blues* on which he combines it with double-timing* in his chase chorus* with Johnny Dodds.

Grandpa's Spells

"Jelly Roll" Morton

50

Grandpa's Spells

13
14
15
16
[A1-2]
mf
1
2
3
(2)
4
5
6
7
8
9
10
11
(1)
12
(1)

[B-1]
mf
(3)
(4)
8

* Simultaneous grace note

(6)
(7)
5
6
7
(8)
8
9
10
(1)
(1)
11
12
13
14
15
16
[C-1]
mf
(9)
1
2
3

(10)
[C-2]
mf

[Introduction]
[A-3]
mf

5 6 7

8 9 10

(11) (12)

14 15 16

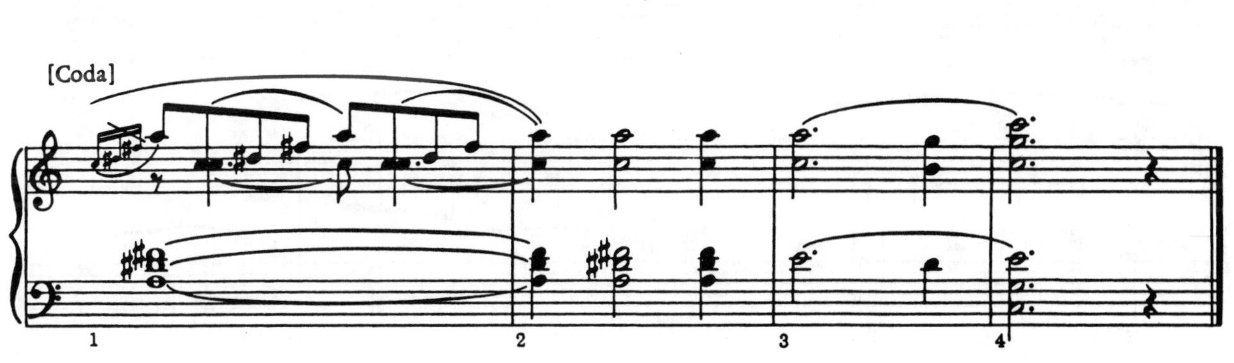

By improvising more variations Morton was able to expand a performance when making a piano roll. He did this on several rolls which were not word rolls. Three of his first-strain variations, [A²-2], and [A³-1], and [A³-2] — the two last choruses — from his *Grandpa's Spells* roll show good early examples of his improvising.

[A^3-1] of piano roll

(19)

[A3-2]
(20)
(21)
(21)
(21)
(20)

On the second take of *Grandpa's Spells,* as recorded by the Red Hot Peppers, Morton varies the right hand's break in measures 7 and 8 of the second strain thus:

1. The C♮'s and C♯'s are struck simultaneously.
2. This tenth is quickly rolled upward.
3. Morton also plays the F above the E, a mistake.
4. Morton seems to falter here, not playing the final phrase according to his own notated version and what he plays in the previous chorus. The reader might wish to substitute measures 13, 14, and 15 of [B-1].
5. Morton plays a wrong chord here. Exactly what he plays is not clear.
6. Morton also plays an A below the B.*
7. Morton also plays a B above the A.*
8. Morton also plays an A above the G♯.
9. This is a cluster of low-register pitches. The printed music at this point says "Crash (Strike bass open handed)."
10. This is what Morton actually played here but he probably intended, as elsewhere where this appears — measure 2 for instance — to play a D above the B♭.
11. A C♯below the upper D♯ also sounds.
12. Morton may not have intended to play these parallel ninths. There should perhaps be just octaves below the upper B and C.
13. A G below the lower A also sounds.
14. A B below the lower C also sounds.
15. The chord also contains a G♮.
16. This chord also contains a middle C and the A a third below, one of the roll's impossible reaches.
17. A B♭ between the C♯'s also plays.
18. The chord also contains a B♭ below middle C.
19. The roll actually plays an E on top rather than F.
20. A D above the lower C — an octave below the highest note — also plays.
21. An A below the B also sounds.

*Although these two sounds are identical it is clear, from other instances of the same figure in the piece, that Morton intended to play what is written in the edition.

WOLVERINE BLUES
originally entitled THE WOLVERINES

COPYRIGHT:

February 14, 1923: lead sheet*, with lyrics "by Ben Spikes, John Spikes, Fred Morton," Melrose Brothers Music Company,
May 10, 1923: printed sheet music; Melrose Brothers Music Company.

RECORDINGS:

*July 18, 1923: piano solo; Gennett 5289 (11546); ♩ = c. 179 increasing to c. 192,
c. May, 1925: Voltaire DeFaut, clarinet solo with Morton, piano; Autograph 623 (792); ♩ = c. 184 increasing to c. 192,
+ July 10, 1927: "Jelly Roll Morton — Piano Solo with Clarinet and Traps"; Victor 21064 (38663-1); ♩ = c. 213 increasing to c. 230,
+ May 21-July, 1938: piano-vocal performance recorded (1675) in the Library of Congress by Alan Lomax; ♩ = c. 153 increasing to c. 169.

Wolverine Blues is fine proof of Morton's talent for creating a series of contrasting textures, each one sweeping the piece on to its strong and climactic close, and creating a beautiful momentum.

Speaking about *Wolverine Blues* to Alan Lomax — as quoted in Lomax's *Mr. Jelly Roll* — Morton said:

> I'm not sore, but I did get hot about how they handled *Wolverine Blues,* which they misnamed because it is not a blues. I first wrote the *Wolverines* in Detroit in the early days. It was just one of those things that float around in my head and one day, when I sit down at the piano, it comes out of my fingers. The first strain was for trumpet (the basis of one of these new tunes of today, *Flat Foot Floogie),* then the trombone strain, then I made a harmony strain for the trio, then I found that a clarinet strain would be very effective, and in the last strain I put all the instruments in the band together and made the piano sound as much like a band as possible. The tune got to be famous around Chicago and Melrose wrote and offered me a $3,000 advance for it. Somehow the Spikes brothers got the letter and jumped up and wrote some words and published my song as written by Spikes-Morton-Spikes. Right there we had an argument, because they just wanted to drag me over the fence, to tell the plain truth. I decided to go on to Chicago and demand that the tune be changed over to my name, when Melrose published it.

As Morton said, the piece must have enjoyed some popularity before his arrival in Chicago. The New Orleans Rhythm Kings recorded it in March 1923, about two months before Morton went to Chicago, and two other recordings of it also predate his arrival there. The lyrics that Morton objected to, those with which the piece was copyrighted, were removed by the Melrose Company, only to be replaced for the sheet music edition — which did not use the second strain and kept the piece entirely in the key of B♭ — by new lyrics, also by the Spikes brothers.

Wolverine Blues

"Jelly Roll" Morton

65

Wolverine Blues

[B]
f
13
14
15
16
1
2
3
4
5
6
7
8
9
10
11
12
13
14
15
16

[A²]

f

(5) (6) (7)

1 2 3 4 5 6 7 8 9 10 11 12 13 14 15 16

[Transition]

(8)

[C-1]

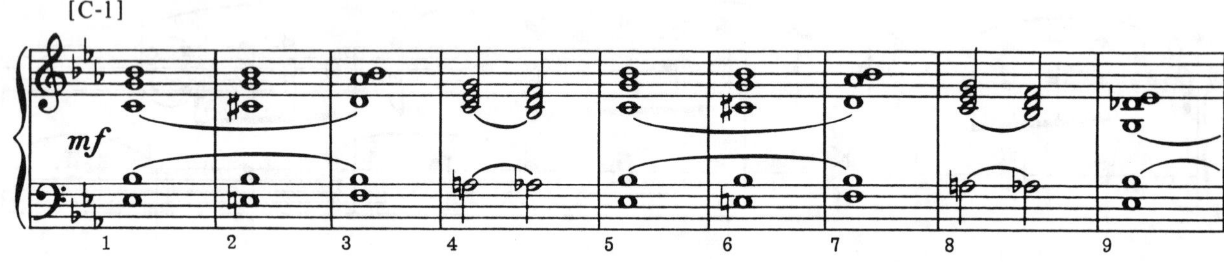

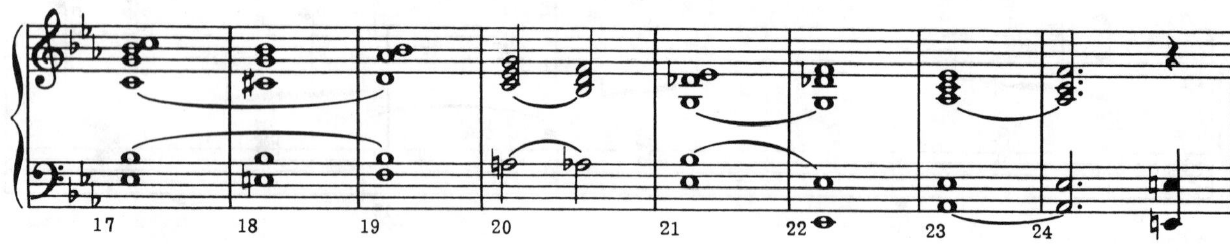

[C-2]
mf
(9)
(10)
(10)

p
mf
f
(11)
15
16
17
18
19
20
21
22
23
24
25
26
27
28
29
30
31
32

[C^3]
1
2
3
4
5
6
(12)
7
8
9
10
11
(13)
12
13
14
15
16

Three of Morton's fine improvisations on the three strains of *Wolverine Blues* are shown below: [B-2] and [A²] from the first Victor trio take and [C-5] from the Library of Congress version.

(18)

[A^2] of trio recording

(19) (20) (21) (22) (23) (24)

[C^{5}] of Library of Congress recording

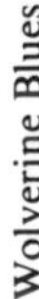

16
17
18
19
20
21
22
23
24
25
26
27
28
29
30
31
32

1. Morton also plays a D between the C and the E♭.
2. Morton actually plays a B♮ as the lower pitch of this interval.
3. What Morton plays here is unclear. This solution is conjectural.
4. Morton actually plays a B♮ here.
5. Morton actually plays a G as the lower note.
6. What Morton plays here is unclear. This solution is conjectural, something Morton typically played in this situation.
7. Here, as in measure seven of [A¹], what Morton plays is unclear. This solution is conjectural.
8. There is also a D between the E♮'s.
9. Morton also strikes a C with the D.
10. Morton plays a C with the D and a B♭ with the C.
11. The top note of this sound is actually a G.
12. There is also an E♮ between the F and the lower D.
13. There is also a C above the lower B♮.
14. The upper note is actually a G.
15. An E♮ between the F and the D♭ also sounds.
16. The top of this three-note group is actually G, instead of or in addition to the upper F.
17. There is some rhythmic uncertainty here, with the G slighted and the B♭ slightly anticipated.
18. This solution is conjectural.
19. A B♭ below the C also sounds.
20. What Morton actually plays here is: 
21. What Morton plays in the left hand in this measure is unclear. This solution is partly conjectural.
22. The lowest note in this chord is actually a B♮.
23. The upper note is actually an E♮.
24. Morton may have meant to play an F at the top of this sound.

MAMANITA

COPYRIGHT:

Not copyrighted during Morton's lifetime.

RECORDINGS:

*April, 1924: piano solo; Paramount 12216 (8072); ♩ = c. 168 decreasing to c. 167,
June 9, 1924: piano solo; Gennett 5632 (11910-A); ♩ = c. 166 decreasing to c. 163,
May 21-July, 1938: piano solo, recorded (1684) in the Library of Congress by Alan Lomax; ♩ = c. 136.

Mamanita, like Morton's later *Sweet Anita Mine,* seems to have been named after Anita Gonzales. It is another of Morton's buoyant, lightly moving, "Spanish tinge*" pieces. A more formal composition than *New Orleans Blues,* it has considerable contrast in its three strains*, with the first strain's breaks, the second's minor key, and the last strain's gentle chromaticism.

Mamanita has similarities to the later *Frances:* it is a three-strain work with the second strain returning to close the piece. The third strain itself is very similar to that of *Frances,* being in the same key and using the same chromatically rising left-hand gesture.

Morton used *Mamanita*'s formal scheme in only two other compositions, *Frances* and *Seattle Hunch.* But neither of them was as successful as *Mamanita* because neither had the interrelationships among strains that *Mamanita* had nor so suitable a second strain for closing the piece.

The key scheme of the piece is unique in Morton's music, as is the structure of the first strain: four four-measure phrases with the first three nearly identical. Here we see again Morton's interrelating of strains. The unique four-measure phrase which ends the first strain returns to become the last phrase of the last strain, where it is also unique by virtue of its being the only four-measure unit. The third strain's reference to the key of C minor in measures 6, 7, and 8 — this mediant relationship is a favorite of Morton's — serves, in the middle of this strain, to recall the second strain.

Mamanita

"Jelly Roll" Morton

[B-1]
mf

[B-2]

(2) *mf*

(1)

(1)

(1)

Mamanita

[C-1]

mf

1 2 3

4 5 6

7 8 9

10 11 12

13 14 (6) 15 16

[C-2]
mf
(4)
(7)

[B2]

mf

1 2 3 4

5 6 7 8

9 10 11

12 13 14

15 16 1 (8) 2

1. An A♯ below the top B♮ also sounds.
2. The rhythm of Morton's right hand in [B-2] is considerably freer than the notation indicates, with most notes attacked slightly earlier than indicated, and the notes being slightly different from each other in time value.
3. Measure 11 and the first half of measure 12 present a confused version of what Morton has played three times before. The reader may wish to substitute the parallel music in [A¹] for this segment.
4. Morton actually plays an E♮ as the lower pitch of this interval.
5. From here to measure 10 the rhythm is again considerably and subtly freer — with many anticipations and delays — than the notation indicates. Measures 7 and 10, containing the same melodic fragment at different pitch levels, have especially subtle rhythms whose effect are heightened by Morton's articulation, in which the highest notes are accented as if they fell on the beat.
6. Morton actually plays a G here, tying it to the G in measure 15.
7. Morton also plays a D between the A♭ and lower C.
8. Morton also restrikes the F a second above the E♭.

FROG-I-MORE RAG,
also known as FROGGIE MOORE *and* SWEETHEART O' MINE

COPYRIGHT:

May 15, 1918: piano solo version, Morton holograph; Ferd Morton,
April 16, 1923 (as *Froggie Moore*): music and words, music by F. Morton, words by Benjamin F. Spikes and John C. Spikes; Spikes Brothers Publishing Company,
June 10, 1926 (as *Sweetheart O' Mine*), lead sheet*, Melrose Brothers Music Company,
August 20, 1926 (as *Sweetheart O' Mine*): orchestration; Melrose Brothers Music Company.

RECORDINGS:

*April-May, 1924 (as *Froggie Moore*): piano solo; Rialto master (534) unissued at the time and issued in 1944 by John Steiner; ♩ = c. 192 increasing to c. 202,
+April 20, 1926 (as *Sweetheart O' Mine*): Vocalion 1019 (C-163); ♩ = c. 183 increasing to c. 211.

Frog-I-More Rag is a warm, forceful composition with rich, varied textures and a wonderful exuberance which focuses on the last characteristically spectacular chorus.

The earliest Morton manuscript in the Library of Congress is Morton's copyright deposit copy of this 1908 piece, submitted in 1918 while Morton was living in Los Angeles. This original manuscript shows this piece as it appears here, not as on Morton's later recording as *Sweetheart O' Mine*—which has a new first strain*—or as it appears in *Sweetheart O' Mine*'s sheet music with the first two strains replaced by a verse* and with lyrics by Walter Melrose. There are several versions of the title and stories about its origin. Research by Michael Montgomery suggests the possibility that the first strain's chromatically rising chords might have been appropriated from a piece or mannerism of pianist Benson "Frog Eye" Moore, a possibility which could help to explain the title. On the other hand, the chromatic idea might simply have reminded Morton of Moore—Morton did name another piece, *King Porter Stomp,* after another fellow pianist, Porter King—and it is hard to imagine that chromatically moving chords as an "idea" have not occurred to many, if not most, jazz pianists. Certainly they occur in other, though later, pieces by Morton, James P. Johnson, Fats Waller, Duke Ellington, and others.

The performance transcribed here has beautiful balance: the composition's structure and overall shape are never obscured yet there is effective use of improvisation. The first strain's chromatically rising chords seem to hold back the energy which is eventually released with the appearance of the two statements of the second strain, and Morton's exciting improvising. The first strain's return, with its braking effect, prepares for the simple, choralelike first appearance of the third strain. The first statement has constant syncopation, seeming to lean forward with anticipation of the first beats of most of its measures. Then, beginning in the thirty-first measure Morton plays a two-measure pick-up figure leading to, indeed exploding into, his beautiful last chorus. This last chorus provides a perfect example of the kind of disciplined improvisation of which Morton was capable—exciting and rhythmically varied but never losing sight of the melody.

Frog-I-More Rag

"Jelly Roll" Morton

f
[B-1]
f

* Simultaneous grace note

[A2]
mf
mf cresc.
a
f
mf

[Transition]
tr
L.H.
[C-1]
(3)
mf
cresc.

* Simultaneous grace note

[C-2]
cresc.
f

18
19
20
21
22
23
24
(6)
25
26
(7)
27
28
29
30
31
32
33
34

Morton's 1926 recording of *Sweetheart O' Mine* is a recording of the same piece with a new first strain. The new strain, its two statements transcribed below, resembles several other sixteen-measure strains of Morton's and eliminates the chromatic material which might by this time—almost twenty years after the piece was composed—have seemed dated.

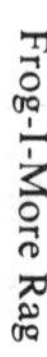

[A-2] of *Sweetheart O' Mine*

1. Here, and in most of the other instances of this E♭ octave, in this piece and in *London Blues* which was recorded in the same session, there is a grace-note effect which sounds as if the D below the top E♭ were being played. Because of its consistency, it seems to me most likely that it was the result of mechanical difficulties with the piano itself.
2. Morton actually plays a G octave a second higher.
3. The left hand is swung in this chorus, following the rhythms of the right hand.
4. Morton actually adds to this chord a rather faint G♭ above the E♭, a mistake.
5. There is also a D♭ above the C, a mistake.
6. Morton also strikes a B♮ below the lower C.
7. A D between the C♭'s also sounds.
8. The left hand in this measure is very difficult to hear. This seems to be what Morton played, but is certainly atypical of what he played in similar situations elsewhere. The reader may wish to substitute the more conventional and more effective music from measure 12 of [A-1].

LONDON BLUES
also known as LONDON CAFÉ BLUES *and* SHOE SHINER'S DRAG

COPYRIGHT:

September 26, 1923: piano solo version, Morton holograph; Melrose Brothers Music Company,
August 15, 1928 (as *Shoe Shiner's Drag*): printed piano solo version; Melrose Brothers Music Company.

RECORDINGS:

July 18, 1923: New Orleans Rhythm Kings, with Morton, piano; Gennett 5221 (11550); ♩ = c. 131,
October, 1923: Jelly Roll Morton's Jazz Band; OKeh 8105 (8499-A); ♩ = c. 129,
*April-May, 1924: piano solo; Rialto unnumbered (535); ♩ = c. 150 increasing to c. 153,
September, 1924: piano roll; Vocalstyle 50479,
+June 11, 1928 (as *Shoe Shiner's Drag*): Jelly Roll Morton's Red Hot Peppers; Victor 21658 (45621-3); ♩ = c. 125 decreasing to 116.

London Blues is one of Morton's better-known compositions, a piece he recorded four times, twice with bands. Other early recordings were by the New Orleans Rhythm Kings and King Oliver's band. The piece's beautiful first chorus melody and its varied textures lend themselves to jazz band as well as to piano solo performance; perhaps this is the reason that the Melrose brothers made it one of the first of their published orchestrations of Morton's music.

It is another of Morton's extended blues* compositions. My designations for the choruses show the basic compositional scheme: two different chorus structures—both blues—in the same key, with paired variations on the first one (labeled A) and single variations on the second one (B). Each chorus ends with the same four-measure phrase.

When he recorded this piece later as *Shoe Shiner's Drag,* Morton made two interesting changes, each in the direction of simplifying the piece. First, he replaced the original introduction with four measures of material already present in the piece, the four measures heard as the first part of [Ac] and as the coda. This is not a big change but it results in a more pleasing and concentrated overall shape. Second, he eliminated the composed variations of the [B] choruses, replacing the entire group of them with two statements of [Bb] and improvised solos, in effect replacing composed variations with improvised ones. (The effect of the repetition of [Bb], played on the Red Hot Peppers' recording first by clarinet then piano, is to point out to the listener that this is a composed, rather than an improvised, melody.)

This edition provides two introductions, the first as Morton recorded it for *London Blues* and the second, in the manner of *Shoe Shiner's Drag,* based on the first four measures of [Ac] and on the coda.

London Blues

* Simultaneous grace note

* Simultaneous grace note

[Ab-2]

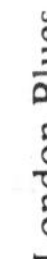

[Ac-1]

* Simultaneous grace note

cresc.
[Ac-2]
(8)
(9)
* Simultaneous grace note

[Ba]

1 2 3 4

5 6 7 8

f

f

9 10 11 12

[Bb]

mf

1 2 3

4 5 6

tr

* Simultaneous grace note

(10)
[Bc]
mf

[Bd]

[Coda]

* Simultaneous grace note

1. Morton also plays a middle C with the two D's.
2. These two measures, the first two measures of the four-measure phrase which ends each chorus, are played differently from the way they are played everywhere else in the piece. Morton seems to have been disoriented momentarily here, as the mistakes show. He would probably have preferred to play, and the reader may wish to play, a more typical version as found in measures 9 to 12 of any of the next choruses.
3. Morton actually plays the lower written B♭ and a B♮ an octave and a minor second above.
4. Morton actually plays the upper written A and a B♭ a seventh below.
5. This is not what Morton played. What appears here on the recording is a strongly played F below middle C. The way it is articulated suggests that it is the missed top note of the tenth shown, played rolled upward. The other, perhaps more typical, usage here would have been for Morton to play an octave E♭.
6. The D below this E♮ also sounds faintly.
7. There is also a D♭ above the top E♭, according to the rest of the piece, a mistake.
8. The top F does not actually sound here but Morton plays it in the other three interior placements of this idea and in the coda where it appears again.
9. Exactly what Morton played in this measure is unclear. The notated solution is partly conjectural.
10. Morton also plays C♯ between the D and B♭.
11. Morton plays a middle C on top instead of or in addition to the D.
12. It is not clear what Morton plays here, though it certainly is not correct. The notation provides what Morton probably intended.
13. There is also a C between the F and G, a mistake.

SHREVEPORT STOMP

COPYRIGHT:

April 1, 1925: orchestration; Melrose Brothers Music Company.

RECORDINGS:

*June 9, 1924: piano solo; Gennett 5590 (11908-A); ♩ = c. 230 increasing to c. 236,
+1924: piano roll; Vocalstyle 50481,
June 11, 1928: Jelly-Roll Morton's Trio; Victor 21658 (45623-1); ♩ = c. 218 increasing to c. 229.

Shreveport Stomp is a particularly strong, fast-paced composition which blends grace and vigor. The tempos at which Morton recorded this piece tend to conceal the fact that the first strain* has a pretty, typically romantic, Morton melody. Like melodies in *Kansas City Stomp* and *The Pearls,* it shows the influence on Morton of the nineteenth-century melodic style he heard at the French Opera. (The first four notes of the melody, incidentally, form a figure which Morton used repeatedly in improvising.)

The second strain is unusual for Morton, or for anyone. A look at Morton's music shows that he was not usually interested in peculiar harmony. But for *Shreveport Stomp* he composed a second strain, fourteen measures long, whose tonal reference point is B-flat major but which refers to the keys G minor, A major, F-sharp major, and eventually B minor before returning to the dominant harmony. This harmonic succession itself—hardly constructed according to usual principles of chord progression—could easily sound garish, as do some other examples of experimental harmony—including some by Morton himself—but there are three main reasons in its obviously careful composition which prevent this.

First, the melody's continuous long line flows over the harmonies as if not taking notice of their unusual succession, and unites the first eight measures into a single unbroken phrase. Second, the voice-leading expressed by the bass line and implied by the melody's approach to major structural points in measures 1 through 8 and its simple statement of them in measures 9 through 13 also serve to smooth the connections, further deemphasizing their unusual quality. Third, the unusual progression itself, in measures 1 to 8, is recapitulated in abbreviated and melodically streamlined form, in measure 9 and 10, and extended further in measures 11 and 12 before cadencing on the dominant in measure 13. The repetition of the progression is a corroborative device, as is the repetition of the whole strain.

The reappearance of the first strain after this unusual second strain shows us how effective the interruption of a first by a second strain can be and, when it is compared with the same event in pieces with similar schemes, how this reappearance can be done to such different effect in pieces with different content.

The third strain's textural variety and subdominant key are typical for Morton's three-strain pieces. So is the fact that it appears to be made for the kind of improvisation which appears at [C-2]: it has a slow-moving melody which lends itself to rather free embellishment.

Shreveport Stomp

"Jelly Roll" Morton

(2)

(3)
(4)
[B-1, B-2]
mf
(5)
(6)
(7)
cresc.
f

[A²]

8

f

(1)

(8)

(9)

(10)

(11)
(12)
17
18
19
20
21
22
23
24
25
26
27
28
29
30
31
32

[Transition]
mf
[C-1]

cresc.

[C-2]

f

(13)

(14)

(15)

(16)

3
16
17
18
19
20
21
22
23
24
25
26
27
28
29
30
31
32

The piano-roll version of *Shreveport Stomp* shows a typical expansion beyond the recorded version. Transcribed below are the three third-strain statements from the roll. They show how the additional time available allowed Morton to use essentially the same material but to pace it differently, creating a more graduated and more effective accumulation of excitement.

[C-2]

1 2 3

4 5 6

7 8 9 10

11 12 13

14 15 (17) 16

Shreveport Stomp

[C-3]

1 2 3

4 5 6 7

8 9 10

11 12 13 14

15 (17) 16 17

Shreveport Stomp

1. Morton actually plays a G octave a second higher.
2. Morton actually plays a D octave a second higher.
3. Morton actually plays a G here.
4. The lower pitch on the recording is an A, not a G.
5. When repeating this strain Morton plays an A octave here, a third higher than the F♯octave.
6. When repeating this strain Morton adds a lower D and plays, by mistake, a C♯under the top D.
7. In both statements of the strain Morton plays an A♯ here.
8. A low F♮ also sounds with the F♯.
9. This chord also contains a lightly played B♮ below middle C.
10. Morton actually plays a D octave a second higher.
11. An E♮ below the F also sounds.
12. The right and left hands are not precisely together here.
13. Morton also plays a D above the lower C.
14. A C♭ above the higher B♭ also sounds.
15. An A♮ below the B♭ also sounds.
16. A G above the higher F also sounds.
17. The left-hand D is a wrong note, probably an editorial insertion.
18. The A♭ is a wrong note.

BIG FOOT HAM
also known as BIG FAT HAM *and* HAM AND EGGS

COPYRIGHT:

August 11, 1923: piano solo version, Morton holograph; Lloyd Smith,
April 2, 1928 (as *Ham and Eggs*): lead sheet*, Morton holograph; Triangle Music Company.

RECORDINGS:

June, 1923: Jelly Roll Marton *(sic)* and His Orchestra; Paramount 12050 (1434-1); ♩ = c. 163 decreasing to c. 159,
*June 9, 1924: piano solo; Gennett 5552 (11912-A); ♩ = c. 192 increasing to c. 199,
March 13, 1928 (as *Ham and Eggs*): Johnny Dunn and his Band, with Morton, piano; Columbia 14358-D (145760-2); ♩ = c. 192.

Big Foot Ham is a vivid piece with unusual vitality and a compelling, unbroken drive to its final cadence. The system of motivic connection among strains*, the piece's variety of textures and placement of breaks*, and unconventional shaping within an apparently conventional three-strain form all contribute to this effect.

Morton makes beautiful use of melodic material for coherence. Measure 15 of the first strain, at the point of a crucial return to tonic harmony, introduces a gesture which is later used as the first measure of the second strain, and as the rhythmic-motivic basis of the whole strain. The break in measures 7 and 8 of the second strain, in both statements of the strain, is a nascent version of the riff* melody of the third strain.

The first strain, twenty measures long, lacks the conventional stridelike* left hand in almost half of its measures, and the second strain—sixteen measures long—with breaks in measures 2, 4, 7 and 8, 10, and 12 has almost none at all. Constant reference to the stridelike left-hand style—and simultaneous avoidance of any reliance on it—sets up the last strain, in which it is the left-hand style used throughout. The appearance of the third strain is also the point at which the piece changes key.

There is a constant building of tension from the beginning of the piece to the end of [A²]. Then the building of tension starts again at the beginning of the third-strain statements where the key changes, abruptly, and the stridelike left hand appears. The riff-like melodic construction of the strain, designed for Morton's powerful variational improvising and the kind of ''orchestral'' piano playing at which he excelled, allows him to unify the group formed by the last four choruses and to bring the piece to a ringing climax with a four-measure ending*.

Three introductions for the piece are shown. The first is what Morton played and contains some mistakes. The second is based on the introduction as it appears in the copyright deposit material. The third is my compromise, designed to have the ascending sweep end on the first beat of the third measure, as Morton's did.

Big Foot Ham

"Jelly Roll" Morton

Big Foot Ham

[B-1]
(3)
1
2
3
4
5
6
7
8
9
10
11
12
13
14
15
16

[B-2]
[A²]

*Simultaneous grace note

*Simultaneous grace note

[C-2]
mf
(9)
f
mf
f
mf
cresc.
(10)
f
mf
(11)

[C-3]
mf
poco cresc.
mf
(12)
f

*Simultaneous grace note

1. Morton may have meant to play an octave C here instead but it is also possible that he had in mind, and partially played, the figure that appears in measure 12 of [A^2].
2. The higher F is faint or nonexistent.
3. An E♮ below the higher F also sounds faintly.
4. This appears to be a nascent version, perhaps a confused one, of what Morton plays in the next measure.
5. A C below the upper D also sounds faintly.
6. Morton probably meant to begin this pick-up figure with a G, as he does in subsequent repetitions of it.
7. Morton actually plays an octave B♮ a second higher.
8. The lower C is very faint and an F below the higher C is also sounded faintly.
9. Morton actually plays an octave C a third lower.
10. Morton actually plays an octave C a third lower.
11. Morton actually plays an octave C a second higher.
12. An E below the higher F also sounds faintly.

TOM CAT BLUES
in a slightly different form known as
MIDNIGHT MAMA

COPYRIGHT:

April 1, 1925: orchestration; Melrose Brothers Music Company.
November 2, 1925 (as *Midnight Mama*): orchestration; Melrose Brothers Music Company.

RECORDINGS:

*June 9, 1924: piano solo; Gennett 5515 (11914); ♩ = c. 160 increasing to c. 164,
1924: piano roll; Vocalstyle Song Roll 12983,
c. December, 1924: King Oliver, cornet solo with Morton, piano; Autograph 617 (687); ♩ = c. 133,
1926 (as *Midnight Mama*): piano roll;[1] QRS 3675,
January 21, 1928 (as *Midnight Mama*): Levee Serenaders (Morton's band with Morton, piano); Vocalion 1154 (C-1630; E-7058); ♩ = c. 93.

Among his own pieces which he recorded in 1923 and 1924 as piano solos, Morton's *Tom Cat Blues* is the simplest. It is, as defined by his performance and by the lyrics which appear on the word roll, a verse* and chorus* popular-song type of piece.

The verse is in the subdominant key of the piece, an unusual relationship. It is a blues* whose melody—a version of the traditional *Nobody Knows The Way I Feel This Morning*—for the first seven measures is composed of three reused one-measure fragments. In the melody the fragments are ordered in this way: the first measure is transposed and varied to become the fourth, the second is repeated as the sixth, and the third measure reappears as the seventh and—

[1]This is a heavily, and poorly, edited roll.

transposed—as the fifth. (A representation of this first seven measures by letter would read: a b c a c b c.) The effect of this is that of a one-measure melodic idea to begin with, then three similar two-measure phrases, a strangely balanced phrase scheme which rather disguises the blues pattern.

The chorus is a sixteen-measure pattern whose first half has a favorite jazz harmonic pattern: it has the same one as that of the first eight measures of *Mr. Jelly Lord*'s chorus, of *Kansas City Stomp*'s first strain*, and *Black Bottom Stomp*'s second (and the chorus of *Sister Kate,* the chorus of Tony Jackson's *Pretty Baby,* the second strains of King Oliver's *Snake Rag* and Duke Ellington's *East St. Louis Toodle-Oo,* the chorus of *Heebie Jeebies,* and dozens of others before and after Morton). Overall the structure of the chorus is like that of a thirty-two measure popular tune with a bridge*—conveniently symbolized AABA—except that in this piece each unit is four rather than eight measures long.

Morton later used the chorus of *Tom Cat Blues* as the basis of the beautiful *Winin' Boy Blues,* a piece whose technical differences from *Tom Cat Blues* are not great but whose effect is very different because of its slower tempo.

Midnight Mama has completely different lyrics from those of *Tom Cat Blues* but is the same in melodic content. An interesting difference of substance though is in the key relationships of their verses and choruses. Assuming that the chorus is the principal key of the piece, the verse of *Midnight Mama* is in the dominant key (B-flat relative to the piece's key of E-flat) and the verse of *Tom Cat Blues* is in the subdominant (B-flat relative to the piece's key of F). Morton preserves this distinction between the pieces in all of his recordings of them.

Tom Cat Blues

"Jelly Roll" Morton

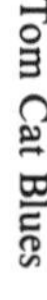

(4)

[Verse-2]

(5)

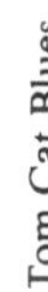

[Chorus-1]

[Chorus-2]
(11)

[Chorus-3]

(12)

(13)

1 2 3 4 5 6 7 8 9 10 11 12 13 14 15 16

[Chorus-4]

1 2 3 4 5 6 7 8 9 10 11 12 13 14 (14) 15 16

[Chorus-5]
R. H.

[Chorus-6]
(15)
(16)

1. Morton actually plays an F a minor second above the lower note.
2. The A♭ is very faint.
3. An E♮ below the higher F also sounds.
4. Morton actually plays a half-note E♮ here.
5. Morton also plays an A below the B♭.
6. This chord also contains a B♮ between the C and the A.
7. This chord also contains a G♯ below the A.
8. This sound is unclear. It may contain a C below middle C.
9. A B♮ sounds immediately after the B♭, probably the result of Morton's finger's slipping.
10. This sound also contains an F above the higher E.
11. Morton actually plays A, rather than G, as the upper note.
12. This interval is played very quietly. It is almost inaudible.
13. Morton actually plays an F as the lower note of this interval.
14. An E above the lower D also sounds.
15. The higher note in this interval is actually a C♯.
16. Morton actually plays the B♮ a minor second below this C.

STRATFORD HUNCH
also known as CHICAGO BREAKDOWN

COPYRIGHT:

January 12, 1926: (as *Chicago Breakdown*): orchestration; Melrose Brothers Music Company.

RECORDINGS:

*June 9, 1924: piano solo; Gennett 5590 (11915-A); ♩ = c. 176 increasing to c.188,
1924: piano roll; Vocalstyle 50485.

Stratford Hunch is an energetic piece with an evenness of expression and technical means that make it almost classical in comparison to such works as *Big Foot Ham.*

The composition shows interesting use and positioning of textural variety among its strains*, as well as harmonic similarities among them.

The introduction (whose absence turns the piece into *Chicago Breakdown*) presents only a hint of the key that the piece is to be in until its end where, at the last possible moment in an eight-measure unit, the dominant chord finally appears.

The first strain's appearance after the introduction changes the texture with the beginning of the stridelike* left hand and more normal right-hand style. This sixteen-measure strain itself has segments of a contrasting texture—repeated left-hand chords accompanying a single-note melody—in measures 5 through 8 and 11 through 14. Thus there are two four-measure sections of contrasting texture, the first one placed at the end of the first half of the strain and the second one placed in the middle of the second half.

The second strain, unlike the first, has similar eight-measure halves: each consists of two measures of a sonorous gesture in parallel tenths, a two-measure break* played in octaves, and four measures of more normal texture.

The third strain presents still another texture—a use of three simultaneous lines—in a worked-out version of Morton's complex improvising style. The two-voice quality of the strain's right hand is most apparent in measures 9 through 11, in which Morton emphasizes the lines' differences of rhythmic character. One line is the slow-moving one beginning on A-natural in measure 1 and the other is the line moving in eighth notes. The strain is Morton's favorite thirty-two measure type for third strains, and he plays a beautiful last chorus on it, one that is—characteristically—both disciplined and free-sounding.

With all the textural variety, the similarities among parts of the piece are all the more interesting. The introduction is a kind of formal and harmonic pun: the idea, at first an introduction to music in B-flat major, reappears to introduce music in E-flat major. Each of the strains prominently features the tonic, dominant, and dominant of the dominant harmonies of its key. The harmonies appear—in the order tonic, dominant of the dominant, dominant—as the harmonic support of the two-measure idea which begins and reappears in the first strain. Then they reappear as the three harmonies—in the order dominant of the dominant, dominant, tonic—which support the initial gesture of the second strain. Finally—in the same order—they appear as the first three harmonies of the third strain.

The use of this progression is especially interesting in the third strain, which is constructed in four eight-measure phrases. The first three phrases begin with this unifying progression and the last phrase ends with it, thereby creating another formal and harmonic pun, turning what was first a beginning progression into a closing one. This interior shifting of ideas is similar to that used in the first strain.

Stratford Hunch

"Jelly Roll" Morton

[B]
f
mf
(2)

f
mf
(3)
[A²]
(4)
(5)

* Simultaneous grace note

[C-1]

(8)

1 2 3

4 5 6 7

8 9 10

11 12 13

14 15 16

(9)

Stratford Hunch

* Simultaneous grace note

1. A C immediately below the top D also sounds.
2. An E♮ immediately below the top F also sounds.
3. An A♭ below the top A♮ also sounds.
4. Morton actually plays a G octave a second higher.
5. The left hand in this measure's second half, which forms parallel ninths with the melody, produces a rather harsh effect. The reader might wish to substitute what Morton plays in measure 9 of this strain.
6. An E♮ below the top F also sounds.
7. Morton also lightly brushes a B♮ below the C.
8. Morton actually plays E♮, a mistake, as the top note.
9. This sound also includes a lightly played E♮.
10. An E♮ below the top F also sounds.
11. The lower note is actually a C.
12. An E♮ below the top F also sounds.

PERFECT RAG
later retitled SPORTING HOUSE RAG

COPYRIGHT:

December 20, 1939 (as *Sporting House Rag*): lead sheet*, Morton holograph; Tempo-Music Publishing Company.

RECORDINGS:

*June 9, 1924: piano solo; Gennett 5486 (11917); ♩ = c. 244 increasing to c. 256,
+December 14, 1939 (as *Sporting House Rag*): piano solo; General master R-2560 first issued in 1979 on Commodore XFL 14942; ♩ = c. 230 increasing to c. 248.

Virtuoso pieces per se are rare in Morton's music—as are novelty, coloristic, exotic, or "modern*" ones—but *Perfect Rag* seems to have been designed to dazzle audiences and to put other pianists in their places, and it must have worked very well. Aside from this, it is also a fine, solid piece with an especially attractive sparkling first-strain melody, and a third-strain melody that recalls the first strain*, and whose rifflike construction gives the work tremendous momentum.

The construction of this piece is less complicated than that of many other Morton three-strain pieces: it does not have a systematic interrelation of ideas or strains and seems to rely on contrast of texture for overall effect.

The first strain's parallel tenths between the melody's high points and the bass line are reminiscent of a similar feature in two other virtuoso jazz piano pieces, James P. Johnson's *Carolina Shout* and Joe Sullivan's *Little Rock Getaway,* but unlike them *Perfect Rag* harmonizes this movement diatonically and continues it for only two and a half measures at each appearance.

The second strain, like the first, is sixteen measures long and is composed of nearly identical halves. It has an interesting "inverted" use of the left hand: since almost the entire strain is composed of breaks*—during which the stridelike* left hand is not used—the place where the break would usually be, the seventh and eighth measures, does use this left-hand style, exactly reversing the most common position of it.

The last strain typically is in the subdominant of the original key. It is characteristic of Morton in its reference to the major mediant key just before the midpoint and its repeated two-measure phrases. This again forecasts what later jazz musicians will come to favor in such a piece as *I Got Rhythm,* another feature that it has in common with other virtuoso pieces (for instance Fats Waller's *Viper's Drag*).

Many of Morton's pieces are difficult to play as he played them because of the full sound he could draw from the piano and because of the relatively long time he held down each key. Each of these features has to do with his apparently rather large hands, evenness of technique, and strength and results in a relaxed but solid effect that is difficult to reproduce. *Perfect Rag* makes additional technical demands of greater quickness and stamina. (The repetition of the transition before [C♭-2] in fact may be as much a physical as an aesthetic necessity.)

Unlike most of Morton's other pieces, which he recorded and rerecorded soon after, this piece was abandoned for a time. Perhaps Morton did not care to record it soon again because most of his other pieces were finer compositions and because this one, dazzling or not, was too closely related to the dated ragtime tradition, which hints at a possible early origin. But in 1939, when assembling a repertory for a set of recordings part of whose interest was to be historical or nostalgic, Morton revived the piece, retitling it *Sporting House Rag* —perhaps another hint at its age.

He recomposed the piece slightly, reharmonizing the first two measures of each half of the first strain and extending the sixteen measures of the strain to twenty by replacing the last four measures with a new eight-measure segment. He also used this new segment in an interesting formal recomposition: the new eight-measure segment ending the first strain also replaces the last half of the second strain in its final statement. Thus the first strain is recalled but not restated in its entirety.

Perfect Rag

"Jelly Roll" Morton

[A1-2]
f
(5)
(6)

(7) (8)

10 11 12

13 14 15 16

(9)

[B-1]

f *mf*

(10)

1 2 3 4

5 6 7 8

(11) (12) (11)

9 10 11 12

[B-2]

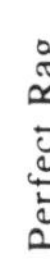

[A²]

f

(13)

(14)

[Transition 1]
[Cª-1]
mf
1
2
3
4
5
6
7
8
9
10
11
12
13
14
15
16

[Cª-2]

mf

1 2 3 4

5 6 7 8

9 10 11 12

13 14 15 16

[Transition 2-1]

f

[C♭-1]
f
(15)
(16)
(17)
(18)

[Transition 2-2]
[C♭-2]
f
(19)
(20)
(21)

Transcribed below is all of *Sporting House Rag* except for the first statements of the second and third strains, each of which is nearly identical with its predecessor in *Perfect Rag*.

Sporting House Rag

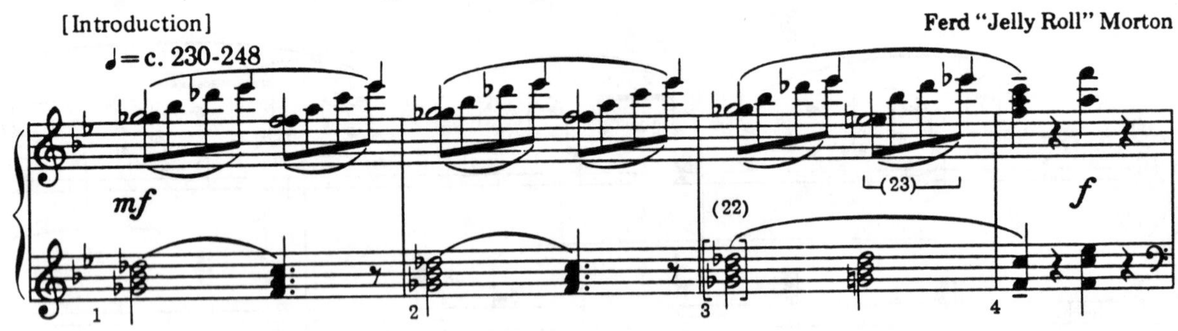

[A-1]
(24)
(25)
(24)
(26)

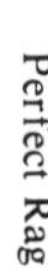

[A-2]

(27)

(28)

(29)

(29)

(30)

(31)

14 15 16

17 18 19 20

[B-2]

f

1 2

3 4 5

6 7 8

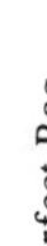

(32)

9 10 11

(33)

12 13 14

(34) (35)

15 16 17

3

18 19 20

[Transition]

(36)

1 2 3 4

[C-2]
(37)
(38)
(39)
(40)
(41)
(42)

[C-3]
(43)
(44)

1. The lower F is faint or absent.
2. Morton actually plays a B♮ here.
3. In addition to these two pitches there is also a B♭ above the A.
4. The higher pitch is actually a C a second below the high D.
5. Morton actually anticipates here what he plays on the next beat, playing only F and D.
6. The lower C is actually not present.
7. Morton also plays a B♮ immediately above the A.
8. Morton actually plays here a single B♭ a ninth below middle C.
9. This sound is very short and rather unclear. It might also contain a C.
10. The lower notes here are very faint.
11. In both of these places the C below middle C also sounds.
12. This sound is quite faint and unclear. This is partly conjecture.
13. This sound also includes a D♭ above the upper C.
14. This sound also includes a B♮ above the lower A.
15. Morton plays a D♭, too, in this chord.
16. Here, and elsewhere where this figure appears, its rhythm is uneven, sometimes approaching two sixteenth notes and an eighth.
17. The rhythm here is rushed.
18. The upper G and an F a second below actually sound here.
19. What Morton actually does here is not clear. This reproduces what he does elsewhere when the same idea occurs.
20. This is uneven. The run following is partly conjectural.
21. The B♭ here is very faint.
22. This chord actually contains no B♭.
23. This group of eighth notes is rushed.
24. The chord arpeggiated above and the restatement of the first strain (see [A-2], mm. 2 and 9) indicate that Morton probably meant to play F♯ rather than F♮ in this interval.
25. This chord also contains an E♮, a mistake.
26. The right hand here is very unclear. This notation may lack some of what Morton actually plays.
27. Morton actually plays the D a second higher.
28. The rhythmic values of this triplet are not actually even.
29. This note is slightly anticipated.
30. This brief segment is very quiet and indistinct.
31. The D is faint or absent.
32. Morton actually plays the A a second higher.
33. Here Morton actually plays a single F a second below the higher notated G♭.
34. The right hand is rather unclear here.
35. An A, a second above, sounds with the G.
36. The F is not actually present.
37. The initial C in this figure is very faint.
38. This arpeggiation is rushed.
39. This figure lags rhythmically.
40. This is actually a C♭.
41. Morton actually plays a cluster of mistakes here, with F as the highest note.
42. An A♮ also sounds above the A♭.
43. A high B♮ sounds with the single D and the C's following.
44. Exactly what Morton plays here is unclear. It seems to include the higher A♮ notated here.

MR. JELLY LORD

COPYRIGHT:

August 20, 1923: melody with piano accompaniment, Morton holograph; Melrose Brothers Music Company,
November 1, 1927: orchestration; Melrose Brothers Music Company.

RECORDINGS:

July 17, 1923: New Orleans Rhythm Kings with Morton, piano; Gennett 5220 (11541-A, -C); ♩ = c. 123 decreasing to c. 120,
April, 1924: Jelly-Roll Morton's Steamboat Four; Carnival 11397 (8065); ♩ = c. 120 increasing to c. 128,
*1924: piano roll; Vocalstyle Song Roll 12973,
February 23, 1926: Jelly-Roll Morton's Incomparables; Gennett 3259 (12467); ♩ = c. 108,
+ June 10, 1927: "Jelly-Roll Morton - Piano solo with Clarinet and Traps"; Victor 21064 (38664-1); ♩ = c. 129 decreasing to c. 120,
January 21, 1928: Levee Serenaders (Morton's band); Vocalion 1154 (C-1632); ♩ = c. 93,
May 21-July, 1938: piano-vocal performance, recorded (1659) in the Library of Congress by Alan Lomax; ♩ = c. 91 increasing to c. 100.

This piece is primarily a song rather than an instrumental piece—Morton's lyrics are his self-advertisement—a piece which he never recorded as a piano solo. As befits a vocal piece, it has pretty melodies for both its verse* and chorus*. Like the other word roll performances, this one adheres rather strictly to the melody for those places, the verses and the first, second, and fifth choruses, for which there are lyrics printed on the roll.

Nevertheless, in spite of having to play a basic melody-and-accompaniment version, Morton has turned this into a solo piece by introducing the kind of melodic, tonal, and textural contrast which is characteristic of his purely instrumental compositions.

The piece, with its verse in the dominant key, already has some tonal contrast, and Morton introduces more by inserting two choruses, the third and fourth, for which there are no lyrics, with melodies and harmonic patterns different from, but related to, those of the vocal choruses. He plays them in the subdominant key, his favorite tonal area for third strains*. Additional interest is provided by the double-time ending.

Since this is the first of the piano rolls transcribed in the volume, I have appended to the music a more literal transcription of the introduction as it appears on the roll. This will show readers the nature and extent of my editing, for this and other rolls.

Mr. Jelly Lord

"Jelly Roll" Morton

8
9
10
11
12
13
14
15
16
(2)
[Chorus 1] In the repetition this chorus is omitted.
1
2
3
4
5
6

[Chorus 2]

Mr. Jelly Lord

[Chorus 3]

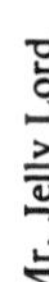

[Chorus 4]
(5)

195

Mr. Jelly Lord

For comparison with the complete word roll transcribed above, the introduction, verse, and only full piano solo chorus—on all of which Morton is accompanied by drummer Baby Dodds playing with brushes—from the Victor trio recording are transcribed below.

[Verse]

[Chorus-Solo]

mf

Clarinet

cresc.

(9)

f

(10)

mf

cresc.

f

1. This and all other left-hand eighth notes preceding first and third beats are played swung.
2. The roll plays G♮ and B♮ between the left-hand E♮'s but Morton does not use them on any of his recordings of the piece. The rhythm here is very square: it should probably be played as swung eighth notes.
3. The roll actually plays middle C and E♭ above instead of this chord.
4. The roll actually plays B♭ and D instead of this chord.
5. The roll plays G♯ and B♮ between the E♮'s in the left hand, and the rhythm is wrong again, as described in note 2 above.
6. Morton also plays an F below the G.
7. This rhythm is rushed.
8. A C♮ below the lower D also sounds.
9. A D♭ below the upper E♭ also sounds.
10. A C♯, rather than C♮, is actually the highest note.

BLACK BOTTOM STOMP
originally entitled QUEEN OF SPADES

COPYRIGHT:

September 25, 1925 (as *Queen of Spades*): orchestration; Melrose Brothers Music Company,
September 18, 1926: orchestration (the same as that for *Queen of Spades*); Melrose Brothers Music Company.

RECORDING:

*September 15, 1926: Jelly Roll Morton's Red Hot Peppers; Victor 20221 (36239-2); ♩ = c. 265 decreasing to c. 248 (Morton's solo at c. 262).

Black Bottom Stomp, a well-known Morton piece because of the Red Hot Peppers' widely known recording of it, is an engaging and boisterous piece. It seems to be the only Morton two-strain* piece other than *Jelly Roll Blues* in which the two strains are nearly equal in importance: it is as if Morton had modified his most often-used three-strain scheme by replacing the first two strains with one strain and composed variations on it.

Each chorus* on the first strain is more rhythmically active than the one preceding it. That this is a composed part of the piece is obvious from the fact that the same variations, in the same order, appear in both printed versions, the piano solo and the orchestration, and that they were also played on Morton's only recording of the piece.

In the printed versions, the second chorus of the second strain, [Bb], is a written-out variation, too, but Morton did not use it verbatim on his band recording. Rather, he had clarinetist, Omer Simeon, improvise something similar, indicating that the textural idea, but not its specific melodic realization, was a part of the piece. Morton used the second strain for the recording's improvised solos, including his own stunning solo, which is appended to the edition given here.

Unfortunately, no Morton solo performance recording of the piece exists. The version printed here is an edited version of the original Melrose solo piano publication. Editorial changes were made to make the original version adhere more closely to Morton's style. Not all editorial changes are identified, but several examples of types of editorial changes are given in the notes.

Black Bottom Stomp

"Jelly Roll" Morton

[Ac]
mf
(3)
L.H.
ossia
f
[Transition]
(4)

[Ba]
(5)
(6)

[Bb]
(7)
D.S. al
(8)

Morton's solo on The Red Peppers' recording of *Black Bottom Stomp*

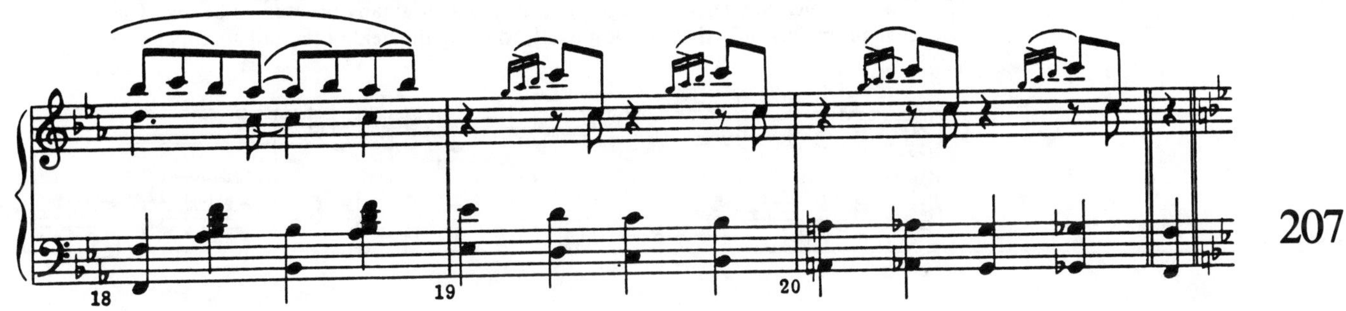

1. The edition supplies a more characteristic left-hand style in the introduction. The original is:

2. The right hand of the original in the first four measures of [Ab] were originally as printed below.

3. The four-measure segment beginning [Ac] was originally notated as below. The edition changes mainly only the notation itself, to make the held notes and accents clearer.

4. Measure 1 of the transition was originally as printed below. The other measures of the edition are similarly altered from the original.

5. The rhythm of the break in measures 7 and 8 of the edition is that used on the Red Hot Peppers' recording. In the original publication it was:

6. These two measures provide a more characteristic Morton-style connection to the next chorus. The original was:

7. The edition provides a more characteristic left-hand realization but maintains the profile of the original's bass line. Measures 1 and 2 of [Bb] of the original are shown below.

8. The strain order of the original at the end is [Ba], [Bb], [Ba], [Bb]. This is not only somewhat unsatisfactory because of ending on [Bb] but is perhaps not what was actually meant, as indicated by the original's peculiarly placed and meaningless double bar at measure 19 of [Ba]. It seems likely that the edition's order is probably what was actually originally intended, a scheme at the end of [Ba], [Bb], [Ba].
9. On the recording Morton plays only the lower F.
10. The left hand in this measure is unclear. This is partly conjectural.
11. Here Morton actually plays an F octave immediately below the G♭ octave on the next beat. What he plays in his right hand suggests that he meant to play, or would have preferred to play, E♭ to E♮, quarter-notes in octaves, on the last two beats of measure 17 moving up to the F octave on the first beat of measure 18.
12. The band enters here, making it difficult to hear exactly what Morton plays.

DEAD MAN BLUES

COPYRIGHT:

July 3, 1926: lead sheet*, with lyrics, "Words by Anita Gonzales, Music by Ferd Jelly Roll Morton"; Melrose Brothers Music Company,
October 6, 1926: printed piano solo version (merely the piano part from the published orchestration); Melrose Brothers Music Company.

RECORDINGS:

July 17, 1926: Edmonia Henderson, vocal, with Morton, piano and others; Vocalion 1043 (C-512/3); ♩ = c. 88 increasing to c. 92,
(+) September 21, 1926: Jelly Roll Morton's Red Hot Peppers; Victor 20252 (36284-1); ♩ = c. 126, +(36284-2); ♩ = c. 123,
*1926: piano roll; QRS 3674.

This is a rather simple but evocative piece. Like most of Morton's more ambitious pieces, it has three distinguishable parts. The first is a quotation from the New Orleans funeral favorite *Flee As A Bird,* a spiritual song by Mrs. S.M.B. Dana. The other parts, as defined by the lyrics, are a verse* and a chorus.* Both are blues* and, a typical Morton touch, they share the same four-measure concluding phrase.

Dead Man Blues

"Jelly Roll" Morton

9
10
11
12
[Verse]
1
2
sim.
3
4
5
6
7
8
9
8
10
(2)
(3)
11
12
3

[Chorus 2]
(3)
[Chorus 3]
(4)
(4)

[Chorus 4]
R. H.

When Morton arranged this piece for the Red Hot Peppers' recording he made a major recasting of the piece, turning it from a mere novelty to a fine blues piece. He omitted the verse but retained the three-strain scheme by adding another blues strain, with a riff melody for clarinet trio. This riff, played first by the clarinets, then by clarinets with trombone, appears after the solos and before the final improvised ensemble chorus, becoming the climax for the performance.

A rendering of this new strain—from the second take of the band recording—for piano appears below. The clarinet parts are transcribed for the right hand, the left hand approximates the band's rhythm section, and the small staff between shows the trombone part played when the strain is repeated.

Piano reduction of second riff chorus from Red Hot Peppers recording (second take)

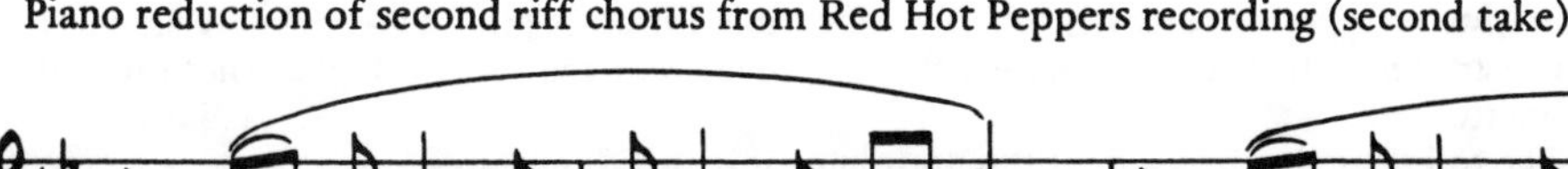

1. This is an uncharacteristic left-hand reach—one that does not seem to appear anywhere else in Morton's playing and is probably impossible for most pianists—probably an editorial construction. In Morton's style either the highest or the second highest note would be omitted.
2. The roll actually plays a G at the bottom of this chord, not an F.
3. The right-hand chord, obviously more than a hand can reach, is an editor's construction. Morton probably played either the top four notes or the bottom three.
4. If Morton played this he probably played it as single notes rather than octaves, most likely using only the lower notes.
5. The right hand here is awkward. The reader may wish to play this as in one of the previous choruses' measure 7, and to substitute for the next, rather static, measure one of the previous eighth measures.
6. This left-hand chord is probably not as Morton played it. It is more likely that he played the chord as it reappears on the fourth beat of the measure.
7. The G should be an F.
8. Morton would have played either the upper D or the B♭ below but not both.

CANNONBALL BLUES

(Charlie Rider, Marty Bloom, Jelly Roll Morton)

COPYRIGHT:

*December 10, 1926: printed piano solo version; Melrose Brothers Music Company.

RECORDING:

(+)December 16, 1926: Jelly Roll Morton's Red Hot Peppers; Victor 20431, Bluebird B-10254 (37258-1, -2); first take: ♩ = c. 140 decreasing to 130, second take: ♩ = c. 112.

What contribution each of the co-composers made to *Cannonball Blues* is not known. Although the piece is effective, it does not rank with Morton's great blues* compositions, and though it is not a very distinctive piece, it made, with Morton's recasting of it, a beautiful band record. When he recorded it Morton discarded much of the detail of the piece as printed, substituting his own details and overall scheme.

The piece has three strains* which are in the usual key relationship: two strains in the same key, then a third strain in the subdominant of the original key. Unlike Morton's major blues compositions, however, this piece has no material interrelating strains, no composed variations—unless [B] is considered a variation of [A], unlikely considering their differences—and no systematic variation in texture except that in the first four measures of [B].

The version printed here is an edited version of the original copyright deposit and publication. The order prescribed by the original music is [A], first ending; [A], second ending; [B], first ending; [B], second ending—which modulates to A♭ from E♭ and adds an unusual three-measure segment to the chorus; [C], repeated; [transition] modulating back to E♭; [A] played to measure eleven where the two-measure [coda] appears. Notes after the music give examples of the editing.

*Not in the original.

When Morton recorded the piece, he omitted the return of [A], removed the "extra" three measures, used improvised solos on the third strain, and recomposed the transition to function as an ending in A♭. This edition provides Morton's ending after the original version for readers who wish to use it. It is to follow immediately after the third strain's second ending.

Cannon Ball Blues

Charlie Rider, Marty Bloom
and "Jelly Roll" Morton

[Introduction]

[B]
pp
melody

[C]
(2)
f
1
2
3
4
5
6
7
8
9
10
11
1.
12
2.
[Transition]
3
(3)
12
1
2

[Alternate ending] to follow second ending of [C]

1. The original sheet music is, uncharacteristically for Morton, too densely spaced in the right hand and too unemphatic in the left. To show the reader how this edition has altered the original publication—throughout—the first six measures of [A] are printed below in their original sheet-music form.

2. If playing this as a solo, Morton would probably have varied the texture here somehow. I have done that by introducing this typical Morton left-hand usage. The original (see example— the first four measures of [C]—below) continued the left-hand style of the earlier strains.

3. The transition was originally more thickly voiced, as below.

4. The original coda, printed below, sounds little like Morton.

BILLY GOAT STOMP

COPYRIGHT:

*June 20, 1927: printed piano solo version; Melrose Brothers Music Company.

RECORDING:

June 7, 1927: Jelly Roll Morton's Red Hot Peppers; Victor 20772 (38628-1); ♩ = c. 213.

Billy Goat Stomp is a very simple piece: it has only two strains*, the first in a major key and the second in the relative minor. The two strains are interestingly related to each other. Each is only eight measures long, has breaks* in its first, third, and fifth measures, and the same harmonic functions in its remaining measures, the dominant in the second, sixth, and seventh measures and the tonic in the fourth and eighth measures.

(Because of the consistent occurrence in pairs of these eight-measure units, it might be that Morton conceived of the chorus as a sixteen-measure unit. But the published version, which Morton might have had a hand in preparing, places the double bars so as to suggest that the eight-measure unit is the chorus.)

The edition is a reprinting of the original Melrose publication, which is also the material by which the piece was copyrighted. Without a Morton solo performance, it is hard to know the solo potential of this simple piece, and because it is less likely than most of the pieces in the volume to be played in solo performance, it is reprinted without any alteration to show the kind of piano arrangements the Melrose company published toward the end of their publishing association with Morton.

Billy Goat Stomp

"Jelly Roll" Morton

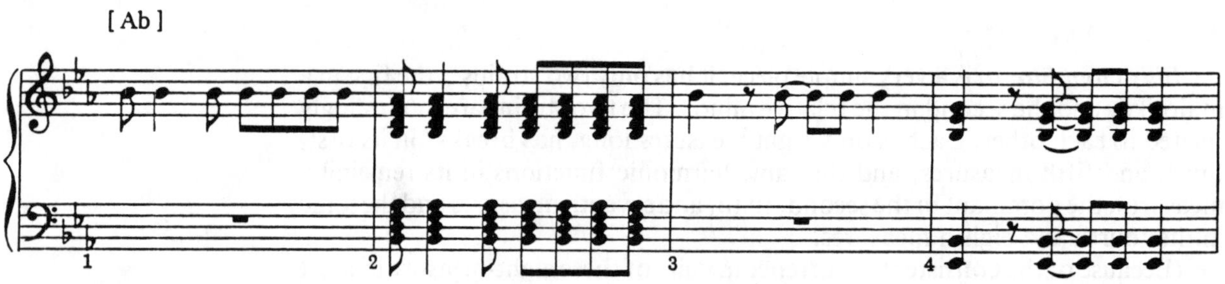

[Ac]
[Ad]
[Ba]

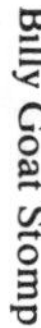

[Bb]

[Bc]

Stomp

1.

Last

WILD MAN BLUES

(Jelly Roll Morton, Louis Armstrong)

originally entitled TED LEWIS BLUES

COPYRIGHT:

February 5, 1927 (as *Ted Lewis Blues*): lead sheet*; Melrose Brothers Music Company,

*June 8, 1927: printed piano solo version; Melrose Brothers Music Company.

RECORDING:

June 4, 1927: Jelly Roll Morton's Red Hot Peppers; Bluebird B-10256 (38629-1); ♩ = c. 172 decreasing to c. 160.

It is interesting to see that, four months before he recorded it, Morton had *Wild Man Blues* worked out in considerable detail. The recording features the band's variety of resources with constant changes of instrumental color. This is encouraged by the structure of the chorus* itself with its sixteen two-measure units, the second, fourth, eighth, tenth, twelfth, thirteenth, and fourteenth all containing breaks*, some composed and some improvised. The version printed here is an edition of the copyright deposit and sheet music.

Armstrong's credit as co-composer of the piece has caused some confusion. A chronology of the piece's copyright, publication, and recording history helps to clear this up.

February 5, 1927: Melrose Brothers Music Company sent in copyright deposit material for *Ted Lewis Blues* by Jelly Roll Morton. This is a lead sheet, with indications for composed and improvised breaks, for the piece as it was to be recorded later by Jelly Roll Morton's Red Hot Peppers under the title *Wild Man Blues.*

April 22, 1927: Johnny Dodds' Black Bottom Stompers, with Louis Armstrong on trumpet, recorded the piece, omitting the verse*, playing the twenty-ninth and thirtieth measures slightly differently, and retitling the piece *Wild Man Blues.*

May 7, 1927: Louis Armstrong's Hot Seven recorded *Wild Man Blues,* using the same arrangement that was used on the Dodds record (and three of the same players).

June 4, 1927: Jelly Roll Morton's Red Hot Peppers recorded the piece in the form outlined on the original lead sheet.

June 8, 1927: Melrose Brothers Music Company copyrighted the piano solo sheet music version of the piece. The cover gave credit for the composition to Morton only, but the inside credits Armstrong, too.

Sometime in 1927: Melrose Brothers issued the orchestration of *Wild Man Blues,* arranged by Tiny Parham. Again the cover credits only Morton, but the parts list Armstrong, too. The first chorus of the arrangement is a rough transcription of Armstrong's first chorus on the Dodds record. At this time it was the Melrose Brothers' policy to issue orchestrations based on issued or about-to-be-issued recordings. It seems that it was this inclusion of Armstrong's improvised solo which earned him co-composer credit for the piece in the minds of the publishers who also wished to take advantage of Armstrong's already great reputation.

Wild Man Blues

"Jelly Roll" Morton and Louis Armstrong

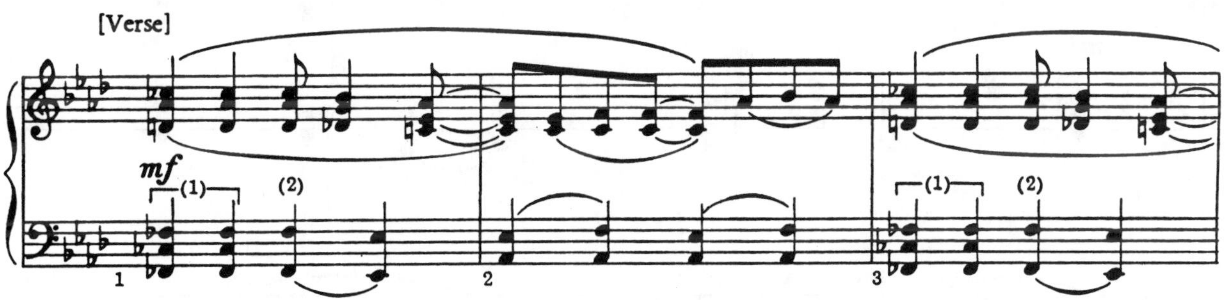

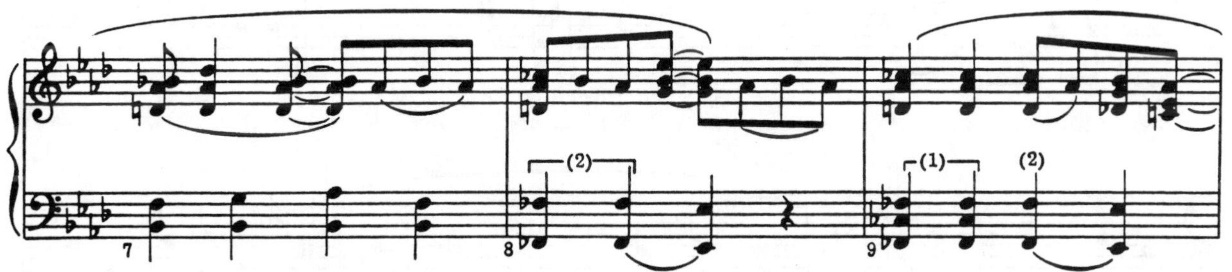

[Chorus]
mf
(3)
(4)
(4)

(5)
(6)
(7)
(8)
1.
2.
(9)
3

1. The left-hand sound was originally spelled with E♮'s and a B♮.
2. This octave was originally spelled with E♮'s.
3. This was originally notated as tied half-notes.
4. The natural sign before the D was omitted in the original, a misprint.
5. The natural sign before the B was originally omitted, a misprint.
6. In the original, the F is left sharp, a misprint.
7. In the original, the E is left flat, a misprint.
8. The E♮ was originally spelled as an F♭.
9. The D♭ was originally a C, probably a misprint, a wrong note in any case.

GEORGIA SWING

COPYRIGHT:

*August 15, 1928: printed piano solo version; Melrose Brothers Music Company,
June 1, 1929: orchestration, Melrose Brothers Music Company.

RECORDING:

(*)June 11, 1928: Jelly Roll Morton's Red Hot Peppers; Victor V-38024 (45619-2); ♩ = c. 201 increasing to c. 217.

Georgia Swing is a light but effective piece constructed almost entirely of riffs*. It is a recomposition of *She's Crying For Me* by New Orleans trombonist Santo Pecora. Pecora's piece was first recorded on January 23, 1925, in New Orleans by the New Orleans Rhythm Kings, and was published by the Melrose company.

Morton's recording sessions while Melrose was his publisher almost always included one piece that was not his composition but which Melrose published. It is likely that in working out his arrangement of *She's Crying For Me,* Morton worked away from Pecora's idea of a medium-tempo, rather easy-going piece and introduced more modern riff construction. He almost completely replaced Pecora's melody in the verse* and abstracted the chorus* melody to become a riff, harmonizing it in three voices. For the last chorus he wrote a new riff chorus, replacing the traditional collective-improvisation ensemble following the solos. All of these changes apparently justified Morton's and Melrose's considering this a new composition.

The edition printed here is—except for the correcting of measures 4, 5, 6, 12, 13, and 14 whose melody was wrong, and some editorial markings—a reprinting of the original publication. The original ended with the second chorus below, the arranger's construction. I have added at the end, as [Chorus-3], a piano reduction of Morton's last chorus as he composed and arranged it for the Red Hot Peppers.

Georgia Swing

"Jelly Roll" Morton and Santo Pecora

[Introduction]

♩=c. 201-217

cym.

f

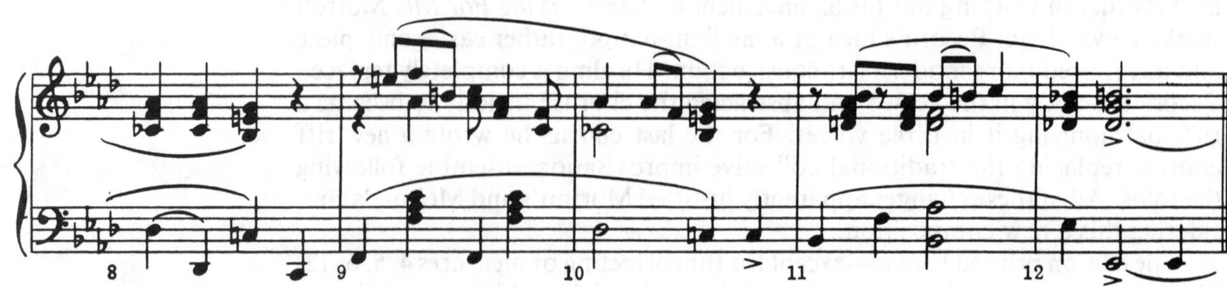

[Chorus 1]
(1)
(2)
[Chorus 2]

[Chorus 3] - Piano reduction of last chorus of Red Hot Peppers recording

1. Printed below is the original published form of measures 4, 5, 6 and 12, 13, 14.

2. Measures 15 and 16 here were indicated in the original as a first ending, and measures 1 and 2 of what I have designated as [Chorus-1] as a second ending, thereby — mistakenly — shortening the repetition of [Chorus-1] to fourteen measures.
3. This was the last measure of the original version. The only difference from what is printed here is that the last octave was an A♭ a fifth lower than the E♭ octave here.

BOOGABOO

COPYRIGHT:

*August 15, 1928: printed piano solo version; Melrose Brothers Music Company.

RECORDING:

June 11, 1928: Jelly Roll Morton's Red Hot Peppers; Victor V-38010 (45622-2); ♩ = c. 106.

Boogaboo is a very simple but effective blues-tinged piece with only a verse* and a chorus*. The two are not very different, the verse strongly resembling the first half of the chorus. (On the only recording of the piece the verse is played, by the trombone, between two statements of the chorus.)

The band recording session from which this piece came produced versions of two of Morton's earlier pieces, *Kansas City Stomp* and *London Blues* retitled *Shoe Shiner's Drag,* and two later ones, *Georgia Swing* and *Boogaboo.* The later pieces seem to have developed as band pieces using the more modern string-of-solos concept. For this reason, they do not make quite so successful transitions into the piano solo medium.

The chorus melody notated here, if not its harmonization, might actually represent Morton's intentions more clearly than does the band recording, which does not present a really clear statement of this or any other melody. Rather, the record concentrated, effectively, on improvised solos. The music here is an edited version of the original publication. The principal change has been the removal of some uncharacteristic pitches from the harmony.

Boogaboo

"Jelly Roll" Morton

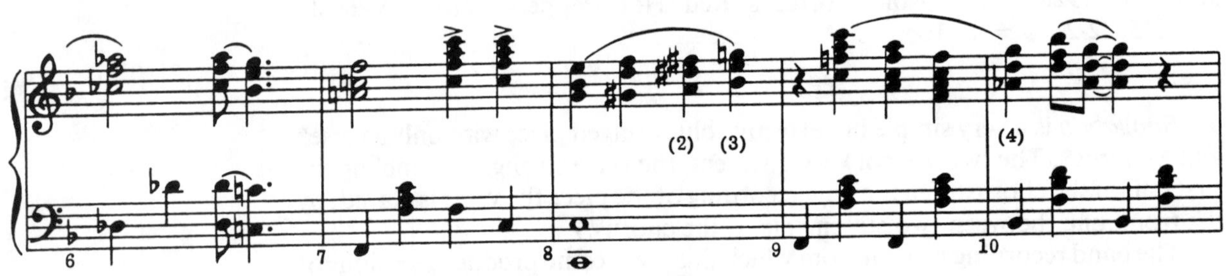

[Chorus]

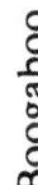

(11)
(12)
(8)
(9)
1.
2.
22
23
24
25
26
27
28
29
30
31
32

1. The middle note of this right-hand chord was originally spelled G♯.
2. The middle note of this right-hand chord was originally spelled D♯.
3. Originally the lowest note in this right-hand chord was G.
4. The right hand of this measure was originally:

5. The D♯'s in both the right and left hands were originally spelled as E♭'s.
6. The original bass note here was C a fifth lower.
7. Originally there were G's between the B♭'s and E's in these chords.
8. The lowest note of this chord was originally a D rather than a C.
9. The C♯ passing-tone was originally spelled as a D♭.
10. The lower notes of the thirds, E and D as in measures 1 and 3 previously, are missing in the original, probably a misprint.
11. In the original there is a G above middle C in this chord.
12. In the original, the G♯ in this chord is spelled A♭.

SEATTLE HUNCH

COPYRIGHT:

September 28, 1929: lead sheet*; Southern Music Publishing Company.

RECORDINGS:

(*)July 8, 1929: piano solo; Victor V-38527 (49449-1); ♩ = c. 163 increasing to c. 184, and *Victor V-27565 (49449-2); ♩ = c. 174 increasing to c. 178.

Seattle Hunch is not as thoroughly unified or well balanced as some other Morton pieces, but has appealing first and second strains*. The third strain—despite its pretty bridge*—is somewhat undistinguished and unlike Morton's usual climactic third strains. The reasons for this have to do with the shape Morton had in mind for the piece: *Seattle Hunch,* like its companion *Frances,* returns the second strain to close the piece, so the third strain need not have the culminating quality which its counterparts in other pieces have.

The second strain has the most colorful harmony in the piece and the only consistent abandonment of the stridelike* left-hand style, features of construction it shares with the second strains of several other Morton pieces. It also has a clear pattern of four-measure phrases. Perhaps because these features prevent a lengthy, unbroken segment of forceful improvisation and because, like the two other strains, this strain is sixteen measures long, it is not so satisfactory a concluding strain. It does not allow Morton to close the performance with his usual very effective improvising.

This performance comes from Morton's 1929 solo recording session—the only time Morton recorded the piece—one in which he made more routine technical mistakes than in others, used a little too much pedal, and even made a few major errors such as, in this piece, lapsing at one point into another piece, *Frances,* the one he was to record next.

Of the four pieces recorded at this session this one, recorded second, is the most tentatively played even though it is also the one played at the slowest tempo. This suggests the possibility that it was not a piece that Morton had fully mastered—or even fully composed—and that he had perhaps only recently composed it.

Seattle Hunch

"Jelly Roll" Morton

[Introduction]

♩= c. 174-178

mf (1) (2)

1 2 3 4

[A¹-1]

mf (3) (1)

1 2 3 4

(4)

5 6 7 8

(5)

9 10 11 12

(6) f

dim.

13 14 15 16

[A^1-2]

mf (7) (1) (8)

1 2 3 4 5 6 7 8 9 (1) 10 11 (9) 3 (10) 12 *f* (3) (11) 13 14 15 16 3

[B1-1]
mf
(12)
(13)
(14)
(15)
(16)

Seattle Hunch

[A2]
(19)
mf
(3) (1)
(20)
f
(21)
(22)

[Transition]

mf

(23)

1 2 3 4

[C-1]

mf

(24)

1 2 3 4

(25)

5 6 7 8

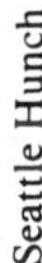

9 10 11 12

cresc.

(26) (27)

13 14 15 16

[C-2]
(28)

[B²]

mf

1 2 3

(29) (30) (31)

4 5 6

7 8 9 10

3

f

11 12 13 14

(32)

15 16 17 18

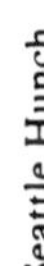

1. The bottom note is actually C♯, not C♮.
2. The chord also contains a G between the F and A♭.
3. A C a second below the upper D also sounds.
4. Morton actually plays an A♮ octave a second lower.
5. Morton also plays an F between the B♭ and the G.
6. A B♮ below the upper C also sounds.
7. Morton actually plays a root position B♭ major triad here, with the lower note of this octave as its lower note.
8. The omission of the upper octave doubling of the melody is atypical. The reader might wish to play this as it appears in measure 10 below.
9. Morton actually plays a D♮ a second higher here.
10. A B♭ above the A♭ also sounds.
11. A B♭ below the upper C also sounds.
12. A G a second above the F also sounds.
13. Morton actually plays a C, not a D, at the top of this chord.
14. An E♮ below the upper F also sounds.
15. Here Morton actually plays a cluster of several notes.
16. Morton actually plays only the upper two notes.
17. This chord also contains a B♮ below the C.
18. An E♮ below the F also sounds.
19. This is where Morton lapses into *Frances* and then, realizing the error, founders momentarily. Measures 1 through 6 are a composite version of this part of the strain based on what Morton does elsewhere. The transcription resumes at measure 7.
20. The upper note is actually a D.
21. A B♮ below the C also sounds.
22. A D♭ below the upper E♭ also sounds.
23. An E♮ sounds with or instead of the lower E♭.
24. Morton actually plays the F a second higher.
25. This note is very faint.
26. The upper note is actually E♮, not E♭.
27. An A♭, E♭, and C also sound.
28. A G below the lower A♭ also sounds.
29. Morton actually plays the D♭ a minor third higher.
30. Morton actually plays a G a second higher.
31. The highest pitch is actually a C.
32. An A♭ also sounds in this chord.

FRANCES
also known as FAT FRANCES

COPYRIGHT:

January 10, 1931: lead sheet*; Southern Music Publishing Company.

RECORDING:

*July 8, 1929: piano solo; Victor V-38627 (49450-2); ♩ = c. 206 increasing to c. 224.

Frances is an engaging, particularly bright and pretty work with three very good, contrasting strains. Like *Seattle Hunch* it was recorded only once. Also like *Seattle Hunch,* it has a compositional scheme in which the second strain* returns to close the piece. (This is a scheme which Morton used in only *Frances, Seattle Hunch,* and *Mamanita.* Some of the reasons for Morton's not having used the scheme more often are explored in the introductory essay to *Seattle Hunch.* Some of the reasons for the scheme's working better in *Mamanita* are explored in the introductory essay for that piece. In any case, Morton recalled and played for Alan Lomax the two other pieces—*Pep* and *Freakish*—from the 1929 solo session, both more conventional three-strain pieces, but not *Seattle Hunch* and *Frances.*)

Morton probably could have revived *Frances* successfully. It is fast-moving and brilliant and is a good realization of Morton's stated belief in band-style jazz piano, manifest not through a transcription for piano of a real or imagined band performance but through constant variety of texture. The piece begins with a homophonic gesture, like a fanfare, and—leading up to it beautifully—repeats it at the middle of the first strain. The second strain has a light solo line for the first ten of its sixteen measures—Morton's reaction to and use of the kind of piano he heard around him in New York. And the third strain has smooth lower-register accompanying lines that are distant from the octave-doubled melody above. The third strain shows still another connection with the earlier *Mamanita:* the third strains of the two pieces are nearly identical.

The last two choruses show the accumulation of excitement typical of Morton performances, with an intensification sixteen measures before the end. With this sixteen-measure strain, Morton's usual four-measure ending is not possible because for a four-measure ending the tonic harmony must appear in the penultimate measure. Morton's accommodation to this, beginning the ending gesture in measure 15 before the tonic harmony reappears, contributes to the overall headlong effect.

CANNON BALL BLUES

JUNGLE BLUES

By

FERD "JELLY ROLL" MORTON

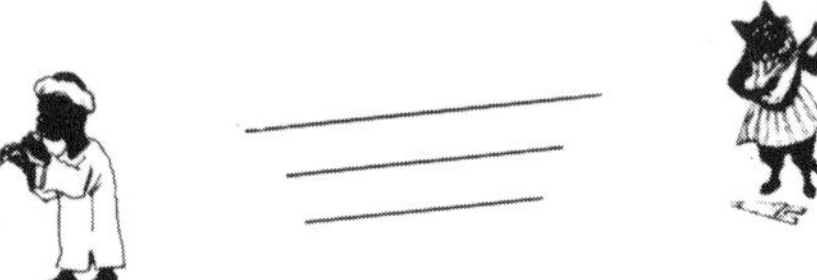

Published by

MELROSE BROS. Chicago

PRINTED IN U. S. A.

Grandpa's Spells
A Stomp.

By Ferd (Jelly Roll) Morton
Writer of Wolverine Blues
Jelly Roll Blues

Intro

8va

8va

8va

Trio

crash

crash.

crash

crash.

crash

Back to Intro, Ending with First Strain.

Frog-i-more Rag

BY Ferd Morton
writer of Jelly Roll Blues

INTRO

1st ending for connection with trio.

2

TRIO

CORNET SOLO

2

London Blues
By Ferd (Jelly Roll) Mor.
Author of Jelly Roll Blues and Wolverine Blues
Loco
Cor
Clar.
1 and 2 Ending
1st and 2nd Ending
Copyright 1923 by Melrose Bros Music Co. Chicago, Ill.
Copyright 1923 Chicago Ill.

HAM & EGGS
By Jelly Roll Morton
LEAD
Copyright 1928 by
Music Pub. Co., Inc.
1653 Broadway, New York.
Same as Big Foot Ham

Frances

(6)
(7)
[A1-2]
(8)
(8)
(9)
(10)

[B¹-1]

mf

(11) (12)

1 2 3

4 5 6

7 8 9

(13)

10 11 12

13 14 15 16

[B1-2]
(14)
(15)
(16)
(17)

[A-2]

f

1 2 3 4

5 6 7 (18)

8 (19) 9 10

11 12 13

14 15 16

[C-1]
mf
(20)
(21)
(22)

[C-2]

f

(23)

[C-3]
(24)
Frances

[B^2-1]

1 2 3 (25)

4 5 6

7 8 9

10 11 12 (26)

13 14 15 (27) 16 (28)

[B2-2]
(29)
(30)
(31)
(32)
(33)
(34)
(35)

1. What Morton plays here is unclear. This is a likely possibility and may be correct.
2. As for note 1.
3. Morton actually plays a G and B♮ a second higher.
4. Only the lower D sounds.
5. Morton actually plays a single E♮ above the lower E♭.
6. This sound is unclear on the recording. It contains other pitch(es) as well, but this is what Morton probably intended.
7. This sound is also unclear. It contains several pitches including F♭ as its top note, but Morton probably intended to play what is written here.
8. A C♯ below the D also sounds in these places.
9. A G between the C and A♭ also sounds.
10. Morton actually plays an A♭ between the E♭'s, not a G.
11. Morton actually plays the G a second above.
12. An A♮ below also sounds with the B♭.
13. Morton actually plays an A♮.
14. Morton also strikes a G with the F.
15. The upper note is actually a C♭.
16. A C below the lower D also sounds.
17. A G above the higher F also sounds.
18. Only the top G♭ sounds.
19. Morton actually plays a G a second above the lower F.
20. A D below the lower E♭ also sounds.
21. What Morton plays here, with B♮ as its top note, is unclear. This chord is what he probably intended.
22. Morton actually plays an A♮.
23. What Morton actually plays here is unclear.
24. A G above the higher F also sounds.
25. A G also sounds with the A♭.
26. The higher pitch is actually F, not E♭.
27. This is unclear, but what Morton probably intended.
28. The upper D♭ is faint or not present.
29. Morton actually plays A♭, not G, between the E♭'s.
30. Morton actually plays a single G above the lower F.
31. Morton actually plays an A♮.
32. Morton actually plays A♭, not G, between the E♭'s.
33. Morton actually plays A♮.
34. A B♭ below the lower C also sounds.
35. The sound, which actually contains a C, is unclear. What is represented is what Morton probably intended.

DIXIE KNOWS

(Mel Stitzel, Jelly Roll Morton)

COPYRIGHT:

November 18, 1930: orchestration; Melrose Brothers Music Company.

RECORDINGS:

No known recordings by Morton.

This edition is an unaltered reprinting of the published piano solo version. It is the last of the Melrose Brothers' copyrights of a Morton piece, perhaps their attempt to use material Morton had submitted to them earlier (by this time Morton's music was almost all copyrighted by Southern Music Publishing Company).

The piece is a single-strain* composition whose structure is like that of the choruses* of many popular tunes, a thirty-two measure chorus with a bridge* (often symbolized AABA). It may not be possible to determine for certain Morton's part in the composition of this piece, if there was any, but the [a]'s—eight-measure segments beginning at measures 1, 9, and 25—resemble rather closely Morton's other pieces *Don't You Leave Me Here* and *Alabama Bound.* As printed here, the music has two choruses, the second a variation of the first.

Dixie Knows

Mel Stitzel and Ferd Morton

[Chorus-1]

♩=c.104-136

[Chorus-2]

KANSAS CITY STOMP
also known as KANSAS CITY STOMPS

COPYRIGHT:

August 20, 1923: piano solo version, Morton holograph; Melrose Brothers Music Company,
February 6, 1925: orchestration; Melrose Brothers Music Company.

RECORDINGS:

+ July 18, 1923: piano solo; Gennett 5218 (11545); ♩ = c. 175 increasing to c. 187,
June 11, 1928: Jelly Roll Morton's Red Hot Peppers; Victor V-38010 (45620-3); ♩ = c. 190,
*May 21-July, 1938: piano solo recorded (1650) in the Library of Congress by Alan Lomax; ♩ = c. 200 increasing to c. 217.

Kansas City Stomp was composed in 1919 and named for the Kansas City Bar in Tijuana. It is one of Morton's several absolutely unqualified compositional successes.

It is also one of only three pieces in this volume which resemble the classical rondo in their return to the opening idea to close the piece, a feature which adds considerably to its exuberant effect.

The first strain is the harmonic and melodic reference point for the piece. Except in the last four measures it has a simple alternation between dominant and tonic harmony. The melody is especially graceful and well constructed around a repeated motive. The second strain introduces pitch variety with the appearance in the harmony of B♮, E♮, and A♮, all secondary leading-tones, and all having the effect of raising pitches of the E♭ major scale basic to the piece. The second strain's melodic line has a narrow range. It focuses on G and its neighbor notes. The breaks* in the two statements of the strain are composed rather than improvised and are effective and dramatic. The third strain's pitch variety is achieved by shifting the tonal balance in the other direction: the subdominant key in which it appears lowers a pitch of the E♭ major scale. The principal element of contrast here is textural, with calm four-measure homophonic phrases answered by exuberant improvised phrases during which the stridelike* left hand reappears. The strain has an interesting relationship with the first strain in that its harmonic pattern seems to be an elaborated version of the first strain's. (In earlier recordings, and in his manuscript, Morton realized the fourteenth measure differently. The version of the third strain he plays here seems to emphasize more its similarity to the first strain.) Morton's band recording of this piece recasts it by ending with the third strain.

The recording transcribed here is a truly fine one overall, but one feature, an especially effective use of a device that Morton uses elsewhere, deserves special mention. As he begins the last statement of the first strain, he improvises a striking melody which seems unrelated to the strain's melody. The improvised line, not a melodic variation, turns into or intersects with the melody in the middle of the fourth measure, forming a beautiful connection and an extremely effective reintroduction of the melody.

The disc on which Morton began this performance ran out as he ended the third appearance of the first strain, and he continued on the next disc by repeating the last four measures, then going on to the third strain. This edition omits the four measures Morton repeated.

Kansas City Stomp

"Jelly Roll" Morton

* Simultaneous grace note

13
14
15
16
[A1 - 2]
1
2
3
4
5
6
7
8
9
10
11
12
13
(5)
14
15
16

[B-1]
mf
(6)

[B-2]
1
2
3
4
5
6
7
8
9
10
11
12
13
14
15
16

[A-2]
f
(7)
(8)
(9)

[C-1]

mf *f*

1 2 3 4

5 6 7

8 9 10

mf

11 12 (10) 13

14 15 16

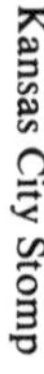

[C-2]

mf

f

1 2 3 4

5 6 7 8

mf

(10)

9 10 11 12

13 14 15 16

[Introduction-2]

8

1 2 3 4

* Simultaneous grace note

[A^3]

f

Morton's 1923 recording of *Kansas City Stomp* contains a rhythmic usage unique in his recordings, the consistent use—over several measures—of the "backward" left hand in the first six measures of [A³]. Here Morton reverses the normal rhythmic positions of strong- and weak-beat sounds, putting the middle-register chords on the first and third beats of the measures and the lower sounds on the second and fourth beats. Transcribed below is the entire last chorus of the record showing that the ending, very similar to what Morton was to play fifteen years later, was a composed part of the piece.

Morton plays, in the Library of Congress version transcribed completely above, a different version of the fourteenth and fifteenth measures from that of his solo and band recordings. Transcribed below is the original version of this same segment—which also corresponds to the music in Morton's manuscript—measures 11 through 16 of [C-2] of the Gennett recording. This is the segment which immediately precedes the chorus transcribed directly above.

[C2] excerpt from Gennett recording

1. This sound also includes an F below the upper G.
2. The lower D is actually not present.
3. This sound also contains an F♯ below the G.
4. The lower C is actually not present.
5. The upper pitch is actually an E♮ instead of the higher D.
6. The upper and lower notes are actually A♮'s.
7. A C below the C♯ also sounds.
8. The lower C is actually not present.
9. At this point the transcription of the second disc begins.
10. The lower two notes are not actually present, apparently an error. Morton does play these same two tenths in the same relationship to each other in the Library of Congress recording of *Fickle Fay Creep,* which he made a little later.
11. The F below the lower G also sounds.

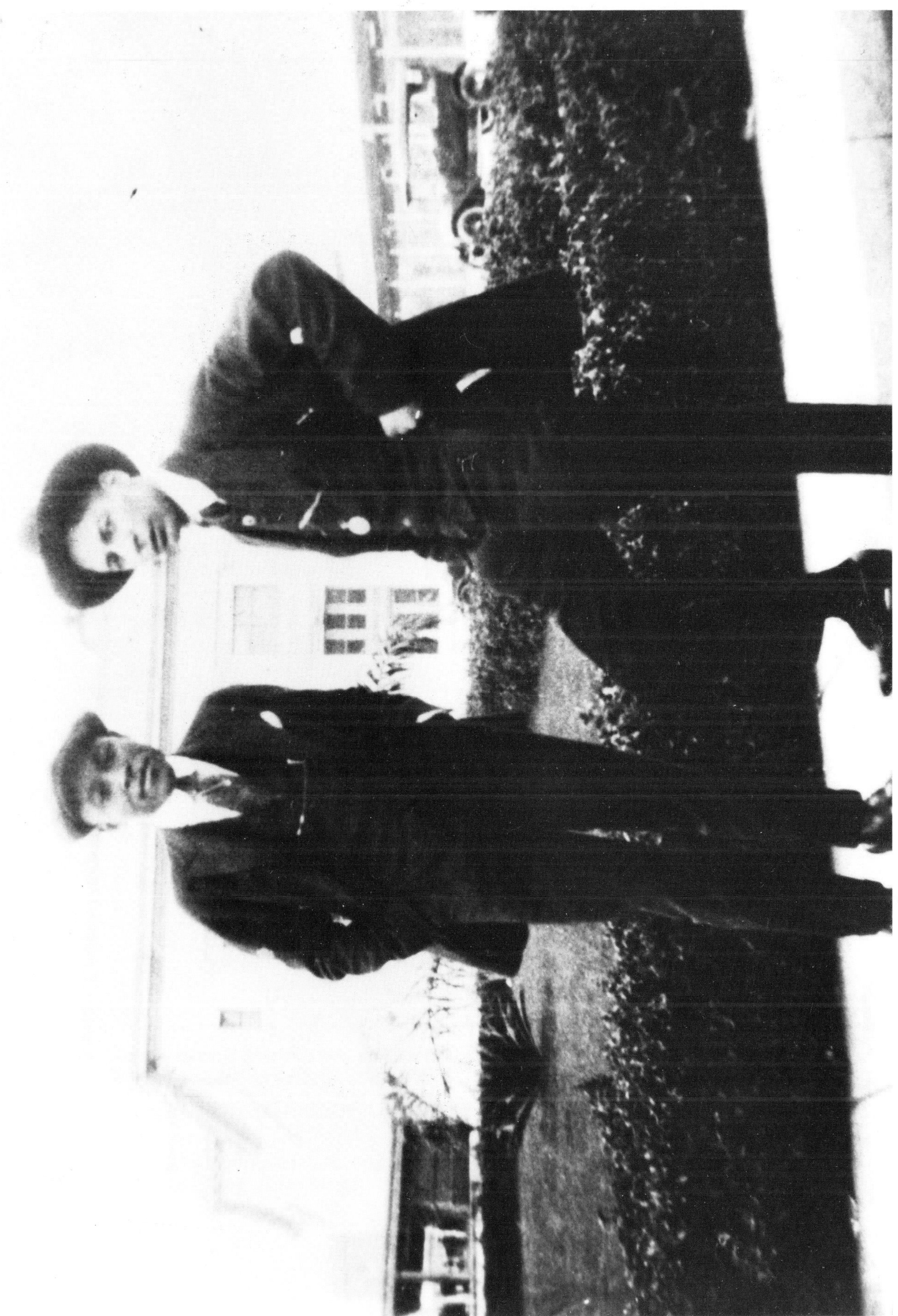

20 CAL 242-515

Mr Jelly Lord

By Ferd (Jelly Roll) Morton

Intro.

Voice.

Chorus.

SPORTING HOUSE RAG

BY JELLY ROLL MORTON

INTRO

8VA

LOCO

(A)

8VA

8

2

(B)

TRIO

Kansas City Stomp

By Ferd (Jelly Roll) Morton
Writer of Wolverine Blues
Jelly Roll Blues

8va CLAR
Sax
CORNET
TROM
8va
8va
8
8
1
2
3
1-
2
TRIO
CLAR
1-
2
D.S.

O K, J.R.M.
June 6, 1938
Bob Peary
Morton
'B'
1
2
'B'
TRIO
Clar.
Clar.
MADE IN U.S.A. by Rayner, Dalheim & Co. Music Engr & Prtrs Chicago
The Pearls.
By Ferd (Jelly Roll) Morton
Writer of Wolverine Blues
Jelly Roll Blues.
Intro
Clar-solo

1-2
CORNET
TRIO
8va
8va
8va
8va
8va
1-2
TR
8va

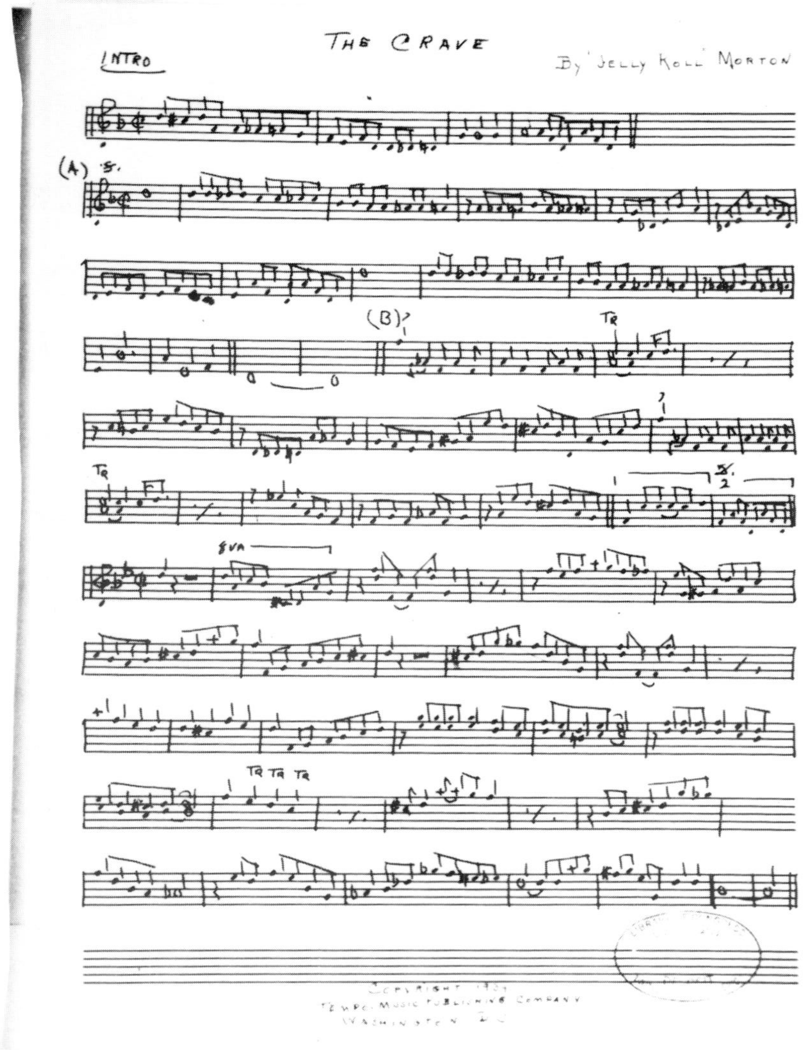
THE CRAVE
By 'Jelly Roll' Morton
INTRO
(A)
(B)
TR
8VA
TR TR TR
COPYRIGHT 193
TEMPO MUSIC PUBLISHING COMPANY
WASHINGTON D.C.

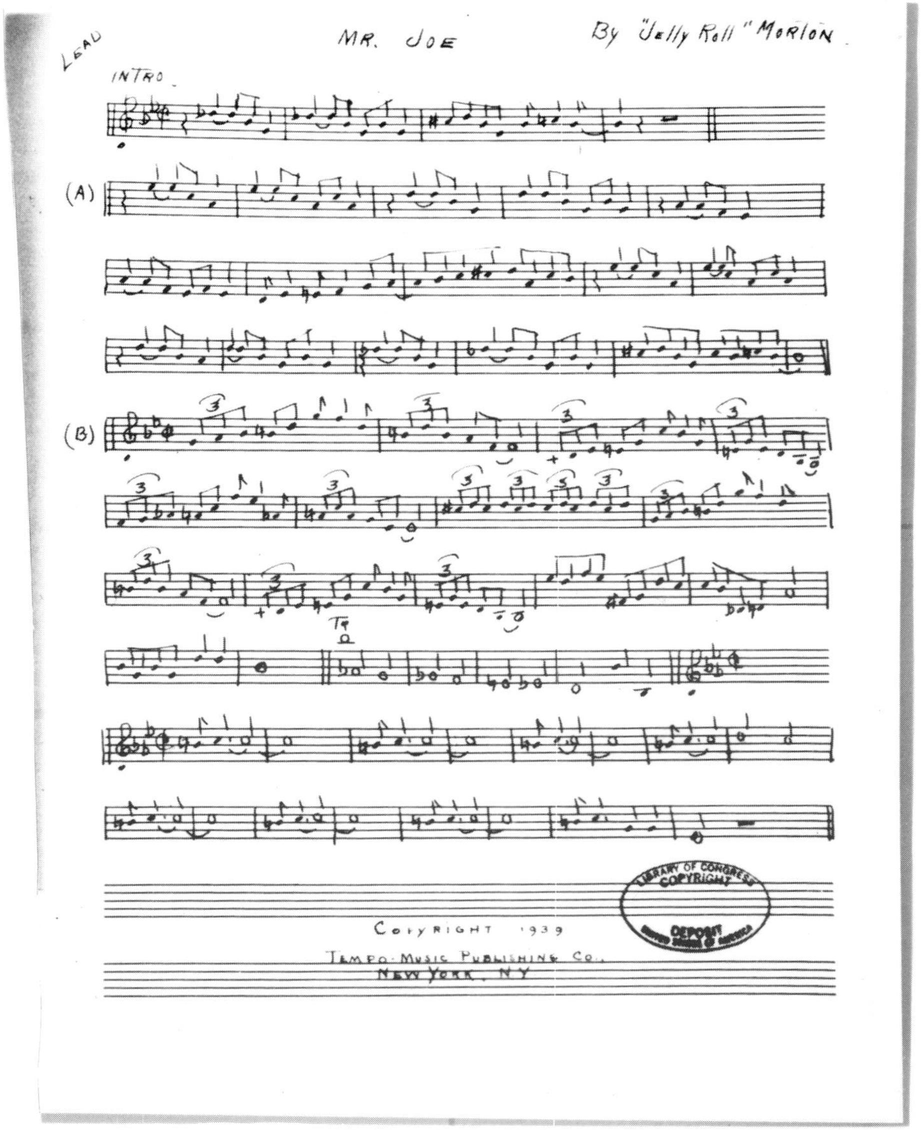
LEAD
MR. JOE
By "Jelly Roll" Morton
INTRO
(A)
(B)
TR
LIBRARY OF CONGRESS
COPYRIGHT
DEPOSIT
COPYRIGHT 1939
TEMPO-MUSIC PUBLISHING CO.
NEW YORK, NY

JELLY ROLL BLUES
also known as ORIGINAL JELLY ROLL BLUES, *originally entitled* CHICAGO BLUES

COPYRIGHT:

September 15, 1915: piano solo version; Will Rossiter.

RECORDINGS:

(*)June 9, 1924: piano solo; Gennett 5552 (11911-A); ♩ = c. 151 increasing to c. 157,
1924: piano roll; Vocalstyle 50505,
December 16, 1926: Jelly Roll Morton's Red Hot Peppers; Victor 20405 (37256-2); ♩ = c. 155 decreasing to c. 147,
April 18, 1928: Frances Hereford, vocal, accompanied by Morton; unissued Gennett master GEX-1202-A,
*May 21-July, 1938: piano-vocal performance, recorded (1659, 1660) in the Library of Congress by Alan Lomax; ♩ = c. 140 increasing to c. 150.

Jelly Roll Blues was composed in 1905, according to Morton, and published in 1915. It is probably the first published jazz composition—as distinct from ragtime or popular music which later came to be performed as jazz—and it achieved enough popularity to be mentioned in the lyrics of Shelton Brooks's 1918 popular song *Darktown Strutters' Ball.* This early piece illustrates the finesse and style which Morton already had achieved by 1905. The vigorous first strain* with composed breaks*—beautifully appropriate for their placement—gives way to the elegantly lyric second strain with one of Morton's prettiest melodies.

Like *Black Bottom Stomp,* the piece has only two strains. The first has composed variations, and the second is designed for improvised variations.

Unlike *Black Bottom Stomp, Jelly Roll Blues* uses the blues* for both its strains. The first strain is distinguished by its harmonic pattern, by each chorus' having composed breaks in its first four measures, and by each chorus' ending with a common three-measure ending. By placing breaks in the first four measures of each chorus, Morton has suggested a four-plus-eight division of the twelve measures of the strain. The second strain has a beautiful melody and a richer harmonic pattern than that of the first strain. Except for the last one, each chorus of this strain uses the "Spanish tinge*" left hand. This strain's construction suggests a six-plus-six measure division. Its performances on the early solo record and on the band recording make this clearer than does this performance.

As on many of his other Library of Congress recordings, Morton improvises beautifully on this one, playing three fine variations on the second strain. He did not play one of his usual culminating last choruses because he proceeded immediately to sing his lyrics for the piece. To provide a conclusion to the performance, I have transcribed the final chorus, another beautiful one, of the 1924 Gennett solo, a performance played at almost the same tempo and in the same character.

(Original) Jelly Roll Blues

[Aa-2]

[Ab-1]

[Ab-2]

[Ac-1]

[Transition]

[B-1]
[B-2]

R. H.
L. H.
[B-3]
(5)
(6)

7
8
9
10
tr
11
12
[B-4]
1
2
3
4
5
6
7
8
(7)
9

3
(8)
(9)
10
11
12
[B-5]
1
2
3
4
5
6
7
8
9
10
11
12

1. The sixteenth note G is held and not released until the middle C is played.
2. In playing this Morton holds the B♮ and plays the C somewhat faintly.
3. An A below the B♭ also sounds faintly.
4. While playing the first eight measures of this chorus, Morton is speaking and here leaves out two beats, the duration of one of these repeated gestures. The edition restores the missing repetition.
5. The upper B♮ and C are actually not present.
6. The upper G is actually not present.
7. Morton actually plays a G♮.
8. At this point the transcription of the Gennett recording begins.
9. An F♯ below the upper G also sounds.

FICKLE FAY CREEP
also known as SOAP SUDS

COPYRIGHT:

December 10, 1930: lead sheet*; Southern Music Publishing Company.

RECORDINGS:

May 12, 1926 (as *Soap Suds*): St. Louis Levee Band, with Morton, piano; OKeh 8404 (9661-A); ♩ = c. 133,
October 9, 1930: Jelly Roll Morton and his Red Hot Peppers; Victor 23019 (64314-1); ♩ = c. 99,
*May 21-July 1938: piano solo, recorded (1673) in the Library of Congress by Alan Lomax; ♩ = c. 136.

Fickle Fay Creep is an attractive piece with a variety of textures, and a subdued, atmospheric second strain*. Morton first recorded the piece in a band performance, using the title *Soap Suds.* Later he recomposed the piece slightly and made another band recording of it, retitling it *Fickle Fay Creep.* When he played it as a solo piano piece for Alan Lomax, he returned to the original form of the piece, different in the fifth through eighth and thirteenth through sixteenth measures of the first strain (which Morton also used as the basis of the introduction on the second band recording) and in measures 11, 12, and 13 of the third strain.

This is one of several pieces credited to Morton that his former business partner Harrison Smith claimed as his own—he said that he and Ben Garrison had written the piece, and that its original title had been *Just A Lonely Echo*—saying that Morton had stolen it.[1] However, the 1926 recording of *Soap Suds* precedes by four years Smith's copyright of *Just A Lonely Echo* and seems even to predate Smith's association with Morton.

[1]Harrison Smith, "Debunking Jelly Roll Morton," *Record Research* (June-July, 1957), p. 5.

The piece is atypical, but like *King Porter Stomp,* in that it is a three-strain composition in which each strain is played, repeated, and then left; and it is unique in that all of its strains are in the same key. The first and third strains recall parts of other Morton compositions: the first has a harmonic pattern like that of the first strain of *Grandpa's Spells,* and the third shares its effective harmonic pattern, a favorite of Morton's, with the first strain of *Kansas City Stomp,* the second strain of *Wolverine Blues,* the third strain of *Mr. Joe,* and the chorus of *Mr. Jelly Lord.* The second strain is unique in Morton's music, an experiment using a tonic pedal and a complete absence of dominant harmony with the right hand's harmonized three-voice texture (which seems somehow more effective on the band recordings). The strain itself is an attractive idea and its appearance, introduced by the vamp*, is arresting. But connecting it, after thirty-four measures of its low-register, static, left-hand figure, to the third strain where the stridelike* left hand resumes—in a higher register—is a difficult effect to achieve. Morton's immediate high-register pick-up figure into the third strain is only partially successful in bridging the two strains, but once he has arrived at the third strain he plays two attractive choruses, the first containing a composed break* which first appeared, played by tenor saxophone, on the recording of *Soap Suds.*

Fickle Fay Creep

"Jelly Roll" Morton

[A-2]
(2)

tr
[Vamp]
mp
[B-1]

[B-2]
f

[C-1]
f dim.
mf
(3)

[C-2]
(4)
(5)

1. What Morton plays here is unclear. It seems to contain a B♭ a ninth below middle C but that does not properly carry out the harmony. What is written here is what Morton plays in similar places elsewhere.
2. A G♭ below the A♭ also sounds quietly.
3. The upper D♮ does not sound.
4. Morton actually plays only the E♭ and a B♮ above.
5. The highest note in this sound is actually an E♭.

JUNGLE BLUES

COPYRIGHT:

June 8, 1927: printed piano solo version; Melrose Brothers Music Company.

RECORDINGS:

June 4, 1927: Jelly Roll Morton's Red Hot Peppers; Victor 21345 (38630-3); ♩ = c. 128 decreasing to c. 123,
*May 21-July, 1938: piano solo, recorded (1673) in the Library of Congress by Alan Lomax; ♩ = c. 117 increasing to c. 125.

Morton achieves compelling and well-controlled variations of tension in this piece, not with complex structure, texture variation, and beautiful melody, but with the simplest blues and jazz motivic material. He showed his fondness for such material by recalling and performing it so touchingly on other Library of Congress records, but here he makes a composer's use of it, showing us another side of the composer of such outwardly more sophisticated pieces as *The Pearls, Shreveport Stomp,* and *The Crave.* While sounding simple to play on the surface, the piece is not easy to play well: it is difficult to maintain momentum through the variations. The piece should not be dismissed as a bit of gimmickry, nor should one be put off by the title—not an especially apt one for a piece so distinctively American—for this is a dramatic piece whose appeal is in its economy of means and in Morton's skill in its use.

After an introduction whose harmony never reappears in the piece, Morton begins with a simple two-measure phrase, slightly varied and much repeated. This part of the composition, [a], is of unusual length, eighteen measures. The very irregularity of length—when we expect units of four and eight measures to make up a chorus*—and the lack of a conclusive ending deprive this initial part of the piece of a time-context into which we can place this simple, two-measure repeated phrase: this is not even jazz's most basic chorus form, the twelve-measure blues*.

The deliberate adherence in this first part to a single "timeless" melodic idea and the left hand's ostinato are Morton's foil for the later increased complexity of the piece. The ostinato continues as an accompaniment, but now there appear three well-differentiated right-hand variations, [b], [c], [d]. Each, like the first section, is constructed of repeated two-measure phrases, and each ends with the same figure. With these distinct variations and the consistently used new closing figure, Morton has defined a succession of closed chorus structures and brought order to an initially "timeless" pattern. His fourth variation, [e], momentarily interrupts the ostinato, providing relief from it at the most effective point—just before the concluding two choruses, which will bring it back. The material of the first of the last choruses, [f-1], somewhat resembles that of the [a] section. Then, a still-calmer last chorus, with the use of the ostinato almost as a fade-out ending, helps to give the performance an overall arch shape.

The reuse of the introduction as an ending on the band recording closes the form of the piece satisfactorily, but the solo version's use of the ostinato alone for two measures at the end, leaving the piece open-ended and functioning as still another reference to the "timeless" quality of the material itself, is a more artistically mature conclusion to the piece.

Jungle Blues

"Jelly Roll" Morton

[b-1]
(3)
(4)

[b-2]
[c-1]

[c-2]

7 8 1 2

3 4 5

6 7 (5) 8 9

[d-1]

(6)

1 2 3 4

5 6 7 8

[d-2]

1 2 3 4

5 6 7 8

[e-1]

8

(7)

1 2 3 4

5 6 7 8

[e-2]

8

(7)

1 2 3 4

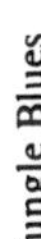

[f-1]

[f-2]

poco rall.

1. This pick-up figure is not actually on the recording, which sounds as if it had been begun after Morton began to play.
2. Throughout the performance there are numerous variations in Morton's articulations of the left-hand ostinato figure. Some of them might be represented thus:

The edition records only the more obvious variations, those of pitch and rhythm of attacks, in the performance of this figure.

3. Morton began this phrase an octave too low to complete the gesture in its proper form, making it necessary to alter the second measure of it. The left hand's breaking of the ostinato pattern is a mistake, too, perhaps as a result of Morton's breaking stride when realizing the mistake he made in his right hand. To correct these the reader may wish to play the right hand of the second half of measure 18 of [a] an octave higher, then to substitute measures 5, 6, and 7 for measures 1, 2, and 3. These, or others of similar effect, are probably those which Morton would have made.
4. The effect of this gesture is always much the same but here, in its first appearance, Morton makes it sound smoother by holding the G as he reattacks the lower B♭.
5. Morton might have preferred, and the reader might prefer, to omit this measure whose inclusion produces a chorus of anomalous length.
6. This tremolo begins slightly after the beat, a D above middle C—certainly inadvertent—sounding quietly before it on the beat.
7. In measures 1 and 2 of [e-1] and [e-2] the left hand, playing a melodic gesture, is swung.

SWEET PETER

COPYRIGHT:

July 8, 1933: lead sheet*; Southern Music Publishing Company.

RECORDINGS:

November 13, 1929: Jelly Roll Morton and His Red Hot Peppers; Victor 23402 (57080-1); ♩ = c. 168,
*May 21-July, 1938: piano solo, recorded (1674) in the Library of Congress by Alan Lomax; ♩ = c. 150.

Sweet Peter, rather like a verse* and chorus* popular-music piece, is not an ambitious composition, but shows Morton writing a more contemporary, light sort of jazz piece, one with two strains*, less textural variety, no built-in breaks*, and a favoring of only one of its strains, the second. The piece is unusual for Morton in that each strain is thirty-two measures long.

The eight-measure introduction, based on the last eight measures of the second strain, is followed by the piece's one unusual feature, the four-measure flourish which introduces the first strain. The first strain sounds as if it were Morton's reworking of the venerable *I Wonder Who's Kissing Her Now.* The second, a thirty-two measure strain which, like the first, is constructed of sixteen-measure halves with similar beginnings and different endings, somewhat resembles, at its beginning, the beginning of *All of Me,* a piece which was copyrighted and became popular two years after Morton recorded *Sweet Peter.* (Morton's recording of his composition, however, was not issued until 1933.)

This is in many ways an unassuming performance, but its evenness, grace, and solidity, and Morton's trombone lines in his left hand—they were actually played by the trombone on the band recording—make it very worthwhile, even in the absence of any extended improvisation. As when he recorded *State and Madison*—and for that reason perhaps producing a similarly small-scale performance—Morton seems to have been playing from the copyright deposit manuscript of the piece. Of all of the copyright deposit manuscripts which Morton and Lomax examined, this is the only one Morton autographed.

Sweet Peter

"Jelly Roll" Morton

326

[A]

1 2 3 4

5 6 7

8 9 10

11 12 13

14 15 16

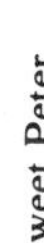

17
18
19
20
21
22
23
24
25
26
27
28
29
30
31
32

[B-1]
(3)

(4)
(5)
(6)

[B-2]
1
2
3
4
5
6
7
8
(7)
9
10
11
12
13
14
15
16
17

18
19
20
21
22
(8)
(9)
23
24
25
26
(10)
27
(11)
(11)
28
29
30
31
32
33
34

1. The upper note is actually G, not F.
2. A C below the lower D also sounds.
3. An F between the G and C also sounds.
4. A C above the B♮ also sounds.
5. A B♭ between the two written notes also sounds.
6. A B♭ below the C also sounds.
7. The lower F is not actually present.
8. The higher note is actually F.
9. The higher note is actually F♯.
10. This sound includes some other pitches.
11. The A♮'s are not actually present in these chords.

HYENA STOMP

COPYRIGHT:

June 27, 1927: printed piano solo version; Melrose Brothers Music Company.

RECORDINGS:

June 4, 1927: Jelly Roll Morton's Red Hot Peppers; Victor 20772 (38627-2); ♩ = c. 191,
*May 21-July, 1938: piano solo recorded (1675) in the Library of Congress by Alan Lomax; ♩ = c. 153.

Hyena Stomp is a beautiful, vigorous work, propelled by Morton's unerring sense of textural balance. The piece has finely graduated levels of activity from chorus to chorus, with the simplest possible full-voiced chordal first chorus and a very complex, texturally active last chorus. Morton's performance of this riff*-type piece has great momentum and coherence in spite of the fact that the first and last choruses are connected not by a straight-line development, but by choruses which project rises and falls in the levels of activity and changes in the kind of activity.

Hyena Stomp seems to be a development of the last strain* of *King Porter Stomp.* Morton has taken a logical next step from his use of rifflike structures for third strains, detaching the structure and using it by itself as the basis for composed variations.

The band recording uses the same variations that are found in the piano performance, but realizes them with the instrumental resources of the group. It is possible to think of the solo piano version of this piece as a reduced version of the band performance, but the solo version, or perhaps even an abstract version conceived independently of any instrumental considerations, might well be the prototype form. In any case, Morton's orchestral piano style not only keeps us from missing the band's color variety, but also achieves a greater concentration on the material itself by not introducing timbral variety which, in a piece constructed like this one, tends to separate rather than to unify the material.

Hyena Stomp

"Jelly Roll" Morton

[b]

[c-1]
(1)
mf
(2)

[c-2]
tr
(3)
(4)
(5)

[d]
(6)
(7)

[e-1]
f
Hyena Stomp

[e-2]

1. Morton actually plays this in these two measures. It contains several mistakes. In the edition the phrase given is based upon other appearances of the same idea.

2. An E♭ between the B♭ and F also sounds.
3. A B♮ immediately above the A also sounds.
4. What Morton plays here is unclear.
5. The lower note is actually an F.
6. The upper note is not present.
7. The middle note is actually A♭, not G.

STATE AND MADISON

(Jelly Roll Morton, Bob Peary, Charles Raymond)

COPYRIGHT:

August 7, 1926: lead sheet*, Morton holograph; Charles Raymond,
April 26, 1928: orchestration; Denton and Haskins.

RECORDING:

*May 21-July, 1938: piano solo recorded (1676) in the Library of Congress by Alan Lomax; ♩ = c. 112 increasing to c. 122.

State and Madison is a leisurely, three-strain* piece with contrast of strains achieved through the chimelike figures of the second strain, Morton's low-register variation of the stridelike* left-hand technique in the third strain (at least in this performance—it may not be a part of the piece), and the gentle four-measure ending.

This is the last of the three collaborative compositions in this volume (not counting *Wild Man Blues,* which, despite its partial credit to Louis Armstrong, seems purely a Morton piece). The copyright deposit is a Morton manuscript but, as with the other collaborative pieces, it is not known for certain what part Morton had in its composition. If it were a matter of the composers' having contributed different strains, Morton's is almost certainly the last, which has the Morton trademarks of rifflike* construction and a reference to the mediant key just before its midpoint.

Morton's performance sounds, from its detail, as if he were playing from his manuscript of twelve years earlier. It gives a clear presentation and repetition of each strain with little elaboration. The performance does not really swing, perhaps because Morton's tempo is leisurely, at best, the slowest for any performance transcribed in this volume.

State and Madison

Ferd Morton, Chas. Raymond and Bob Peary

346

[A-2]
(3)
(4)

[B-1]
L. H.
L. H.
(5)
(6)

[B-2]

L. H.

(7)

(8)

1 2 3 4 5

6 7 8 9

10 11 12

13 14 15 16

[Transition]

1 2 3 4

[C-1]

[C-2]
(10)
(12)
(13)

1. A B♭ below middle C also sounds in this chord.
2. Morton also plays a C with the B.
3. A D between the E and C also sounds.
4. The lower note of this interval is actually a D.
5. A G sounds with this A.
6. Morton actually plays an E.
7. Morton actually plays a B.
8. Morton actually plays an F.
9. What Morton actually plays is somewhat confused. The edition provides a solution based partly on Morton's notated version and partly on what he plays in [C-2]. Morton actually plays:

10. This is perplexing. In these places Morton plays what sounds like an E♭ major triad, that is the G written here and the E♭ below it and the B♭ above. This certainly does not fit the harmonic implications at these points but Morton repeats it. What I have written in is what Morton does in other places in which he uses this left-hand technique and this harmony.
11. A fairly audible C above middle C also sounds here, which Morton could easily have played but probably did not, it being the result instead of the acoustical situation generated by the F and C below.
12. The rhythm here is actually more like that of dotted eighth and sixteenth notes.
13. This octave is lightly rolled, upward.

BERT WILLIAMS

COPYRIGHT:

Not copyrighted during Morton's lifetime.

RECORDING:

*May 21-July, 1938: piano solo, recorded (1678) in the Library of Congress by Alan Lomax; ♩ = c. 163 increasing to c. 169.

Bert Williams is a graceful, sophisticated three-strain* composition. According to *They All Played Ragtime* by Rudi Blesh and Harriet Janis,[1] this fine piece, which might have been lost had Morton not recalled and played it for Lomax, was composed in 1911 and named for vaudeville comedian Bert Williams after Williams had heard and admired it.

The first strain's attractive repeated gesture descending through three octaves carries with it a pun in the form of a harmony which is resolved first to the dominant harmony then, respelled—the A♭ changed to G♯—to the tonic harmony. The second strain itself is not a very distinguished idea, but Morton's playing of it shows the function of such an idea in the whole scheme of the piece: from the relative calm of the beginning of the first statement of the second strain —a marked decrease of activity from the previously ended chorus—Morton builds to the jingling, active texture at the end of the second statement of the second strain, making an increase of activity which serves to introduce the reappearance of the first strain. The third strain, like the first, contains textural contrast within it. Morton takes advantage of this by playing the opening gesture substantially the same way each time it appears (except the seventh) and improvising variations on the material surrounding this fixed idea.

[1]Rudi Blesh and Harriet Janis, *They All Played Ragtime* (New York: Alfred A. Knopf, 1950).

Bert Williams

"Jelly Roll" Morton

[A^{1}-2]

[B-1]
(6)
mf cresc.
f

[B-2]

mf cresc.

1 2 3

4 5 6

7 8 9

f

3

10 11 12

13 14 15 16

[A2-1]

[C-1]
f
(7)

[C-2]
f
dim.
mf
3
(8)
1
2
3
4
5
6
7
8
9
10
11
12
13
14
15
16

[C-3]

(9) (10) (11) (12)

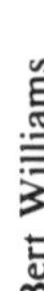

[C-4]
(13)
(14)

1. Morton actually plays a G followed by an F rather than F followed by E.
2. An E below the F also sounds.
3. A B♮ below the C also sounds.
4. An E below the F and a C below the D also sound.
5. Morton makes several mistakes here, actually playing:

6. A D sounds with the C♯.
7. The higher note is actually a D♮ a second below the written E♮.
8. The lower pitch is actually B♮.
9. Morton actually plays a B♮ octave.
10. The higher pitch is actually an F♯.
11. These notes are very faint.
12. This is conjectural. What Morton actually plays here is unclear.
13. The lower pitch is not actually present.
14. This chord also contains an A♮.

FREAKISH

COPYRIGHT:

September 28, 1929: lead sheet*; Southern Music Publishing Company.

RECORDINGS:

July 8, 1929: piano solo; Victor 27565 (49451-1); ♩ = c. 165 increasing to c. 196, and Victor V-38527 (49451-2); ♩ = c. 182 increasing to c. 202.
*May 21-July, 1938: piano solo, recorded (1678) in the Library of Congress by Alan Lomax; ♩ = c. 157 increasing to c. 161.

Freakish was first recorded in 1929, about a year and a half after Morton had moved to New York, and shows him giving in to the temptation to write a "modern"* piece. For this reason, this is one of the most dated of Morton's pieces, because, in answering the immediate concerns of being "modern," Morton adopted the usages that were the first to be discarded when a new modernism superseded this one.

To show that he was keeping up, Morton used, in the introduction, first strain,* and coda, ninth chords (in this case the dominant major-ninth form) in parallel motion, constructing homophonic gestures with them which systematically brought about cross relations—the effect the title undoubtedly alludes to. In this, Morton did what others had done and would do to achieve a new harmonic style, and in it he constructed a piece which succeeded as well as many of its type. The problem was that once such a passage was over—and music such as the first four measures of the first strain could not be made to go on for long—the composer had to lapse back into a more normal tonal style. Since none of the prevailing jazz styles could integrate this kind of "modern" music into its normal *modus operandi,* it automatically produced a somewhat musically schizophrenic effect.

Nevertheless, *Freakish,* like the better pieces of its type, has momentum and vitality. Its success lies in the extent—a considerable one—to which Morton's personality comes through and in the variety afforded by its being another piece with a classic three-strain scheme, a scheme it shares with many other "modern" pieces, most of which were written by composer-pianists of Morton's generation who had similar grounding in ragtime.

The first strain alternates its four-measure "modern" phrases with those more characteristic of Morton, phrases whose harmonic outlines Morton and others had used before. This strain has an interesting phrase structure: it has melodic units of four measures, four measures, six measures (the unconventional length being the result of its being conceptually a four-measure phrase with its last two measures repeated), and four measures, making an unusual total length of twenty-two measures.

The second strain continues the idea of harmonies in parallel motion but this time, with dominant seventh-type chords descending chromatically to the dominant, a sound much nearer to Morton's normal style results.

The third strain is a favorite type for Morton, a sixteen-measure structure containing, just before the midpoint, a reference to the mediant key, D minor. Ironically, considering Morton's intentions, it is this more purely Morton-styled strain which is most enduringly modern in conception: its use of repeated two-measure phrases, a kind of structure that Morton pioneered in his earliest pieces, became an increasingly used device for building jazz pieces from this time onward.

The piece is represented here by a transcription of the Library of Congress performance of it, which is better than the earlier recordings in that it is a full statement of the piece (the second Victor take is not: it omits the repetition of the first strain), it contains improvising on the third strain (not in the first Victor take), and it does not rush as much as both of the Victor takes do.

Freakish

"Jelly Roll" Morton

[Introduction]

♩=c.157-161

[A1- 2]

*Simultaneous grace note

[B-1]

[B-2]

[A2]
(10)
(11)

Transition

[C - 1]

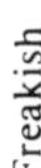

* Simultaneous grace note

(13)
(14)
[C - 2]
(15)
(16)

(17)
(18)
tr
[C - 3]

8
9
10

11
12
13

14
15
16

1
2
3
4

1. The top C does not sound.
2. Morton actually plays a C♯ rather than a C at the top of this chord.
3. The G does not sound on the recording.
4. Morton also plays a B♮ with the A.
5. What Morton plays here is unclear. This is conjectural but may be what he actually played.
6. Morton actually plays a B♮.
7. The upper two notes are actually G♯ moving to A rather than F♯ to G.
8. An F above the E also sounds.
9. E is also struck with the F.
10. Morton falters slightly playing this atypical left-hand figure.
11. Morton actually plays a D.
12. The top D does not sound here but Morton plays it everywhere else where this figure appears.
13. The upper G does not sound.
14. A C between the F and D also sounds.
15. The rhythm of this triplet is distorted.
16. The rhythm of the right hand from here to the middle of measure 8 is an approximation.
17. Because of the extreme shortness of Morton's articulation of his left hand, it is very difficult to hear the left-hand pitches. This is a conjectural solution.
18. The two right-hand lines are not precisely rhythmically together.

PEP

COPYRIGHT:

December 10, 1931: lead sheet*; Southern Music Publishing Company.

RECORDINGS:

+ July 8, 1929: piano solo; Victor V-38627 (49448-2); ♩ = c. 198 increasing to c. 208,
*May 21-July, 1938: piano solo, recorded (1679) in the Library of Congress by Alan Lomax; ♩ = c. 192 increasing to c. 215.

Pep is an attractive, vigorous piece with well-balanced contrasts of texture and harmonic content.

The piece is a companion in time, and perhaps somewhat in conception, as well, to *Freakish.* In fact *Pep*'s first strain* is very similar to the first strain of *Freakish.* Considering these similarities, it is interesting to see the means by which Morton manages to keep them differentiated from each other. *Pep* is a less obvious attempt at modernity, with only dominant-seventh type chords descending chromatically in the first strain, which makes it much less dated than *Freakish.*

The second strain begins with a harmonic progression which is not "modern" but which carries out the piece's initial idea of using interesting harmony and does it at a point which also introduces textural contrast. The third strain is a typical Morton thirty-two-measure structure, one which closely resembles the third strains of *Shreveport Stomp* and *Stratford Hunch* and which Morton uses similarly to improvise variations to close the performance.

The Victor performance is very good, and rushes less than the one transcribed here. But this performance has a more effective accumulation of energy at the beginning, with Morton's withholding of the stridelike left hand until the second appearance of the first strain, a finer increase of tension in the presentations of the second strain, and an additional chorus of improvisation on the third strain at the end.

The last chorus of the Victor version, a fine improvisation, is shown at the end of the complete Library of Congress version.

Pep

380

"Jelly Roll" Morton

[A^1 - 2]

f

(2) (3) (4) (5) (6) (7)

1 2 3 4 5 6 7 8 9 10 11 12 13 14 15 16

382

[B - 2]

mf cresc.

383

1 2 3

4 5 *f* 6

7 (11) 8 (12) 9

Pep

10 11 12

13 14 15 (13) 16 (14)

Pep

[Transition]

[C - 1]

mf

(19)

[C - 2]

Pep

Pep

[C - 3]
(21)
(22)

[C - 2] of Victor recording
f
(26)
(27)
(28)
(29)
(30)
(31)
31
32
1
2
3
4
5
6
7
8
9
10
11
12
13
14
15
16
17
18
Pep

1. The bottom pitch is actually an E♮.
2. Morton actually plays an F octave a second higher.
3. Morton actually plays a D a second above the written C.
4. In this half measure Morton actually plays:

5. The upper note is actually an E♭ a second below the higher written F.
6. A B♮ below also sounds with the C.
7. Morton actually plays a B♮.
8. Morton plays only the B♭.
9. Morton actually plays a D a second above the written C.
10. A G sounds with the F.
11. Morton actually plays D above middle C and B♮ and G below.
12. Morton actually plays a D octave a second higher.
13. Morton actually plays a D a second above the written C.
14. Morton actually plays an F♯ octave a second below.
15. A B♮ sounds with the A.
16. The G is not actually present.
17. Morton makes several mistakes in this ascending figure. The edition provides a likely version of what Morton attempted.
18. Morton actually played G and B♮, a second higher than the F and A written.
19. These notes are very faint.
20. Morton actually plays middle C and the B♭ below.
21. Morton actually plays an A octave a second higher.
22. The higher pitch is actually a B♮.
23. This is a conjectural solution. What Morton actually played, containing an E♭, is not clear.
24. Morton also plays a D between the G and the C.
25. This is conjectural. What Morton plays is unclear.
26. An A above the upper G also sounds.
27. A D above the upper C also sounds.
28. A G♯ below the upper A also sounds.
29. A D above the C also sounds. Morton probably intended to play the chord as it appears on the fourth beat of this measure.
30. Morton actually plays a D a second above this C.
31. What Morton plays here is unclear. It contains or might be only:

32. Morton actually plays an A a second above.
33. An A above the upper G also sounds.

CREEPY FEELING

COPYRIGHT:

Not copyrighted during Morton's lifetime.

RECORDINGS:

*May 21-July, 1938: piano solo, recorded (1683) in the Library of Congress by Alan Lomax; ♩ = c. 130 increasing to c. 133.
December, 1938: piano solo; Jazzman 12 (MLB-146); ♩ = c. 162.

Creepy Feeling is a fine, large-scale, "Spanish tinge*" piece, a beautifully composed piece which Morton also performs beautifully.

The piece has an unusual key scheme with its three strains* in F minor, C major and E♭ major respectively. Also relatively rare for Morton is the first strain's return to close the piece, and the structure of the third strain itself, two sixteen-measure units very different from each other (of all the music in this volume only the third strain of *The Crave,* another ambitious three-strain Spanish tinge piece, is similarly constructed).

The impression the piece gives of being a unified work, despite its size and this extended performance of it, makes examination of some of its features worthwhile, particularly as regards similarities and interrelationships among sections. The first half of the first strain—the first eight measures—resembles, in terms of harmonic function if not in texture, the first quarter of the third strain—the first eight measures. Specifically, there are four measures of tonic harmony, two of a diversion—principally to the dominant harmony—then two measures of tonic harmony. The difference, of course, is that in the first strain the tonic harmony is F minor and in the third strain it is E♭ major.

Another interesting relationship is in the references to G major: they appear in both the second (m. 5 *et seq.*) and third (m. 13 *et seq.*) strains just before mid-point. Thus Morton is using a relationship based not upon the same harmonic function, tonic and dominant, but upon the same harmony itself, G major, which is temporarily heard as a tonic. (As an additional relationship Morton uses at this point in the third strain gestures recalling the *beginning* of the second strain.) A further relationship is that the second and third strains end with similar harmonic patterns which take up the last quarter of each strain's length. However since the third strain is twice as long as the second, this pattern is proportionally expanded in its second appearance to take twice as long to be completed.

Another organizational element is that Morton tends to play the second and third strains, which of course are separated by an appearance of the first, with two simulaneous right-hand lines and the first strain with a single line, further differentiating by texture the parts of the piece.

Aside from the fact that this is an interesting piece, the performance of it shows the fineness and control of Morton's playing more clearly and at greater length than do others transcribed here. Morton's touch is light and never forced even when he plays accents. He plays several segments of particular beauty merely from the pianistic point of view, including measures 5 to 8 of [B-2] and measures 25 to 28 of [C-2].

This performance was recorded on two sides of a disc. The transcription of the first side ends at measure 17 of [C-1], omitting the music at the end of the first side. Measure 17 of [C-1] begins the transcription of the second side, omitting the first sixteen measures in order to join the two halves of the third strain.

Creepy Feeling

[A1-2]
mf
(3)
(4)
mp

[B-1]
mf

[B-2]
ossia:

(7)
[A-2]

[C-1]
mp
mf

18
19
20
21
22
23
24
25
26
27
28
29
(10)
30
31
32
(11)

[C-2]
1
2
3
4
5
6
7
8
9
10
11
12
(12)
3
tr
13
14
15
16

[C-3]
mp
mf

mp
tr
cresc.
mf
tr
tr

[Transition]
p
[A3-1]
tr
mp

mf

[A3-2]

cresc.

(15)

f dim.

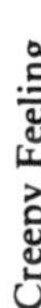

mf
[A3-3]
mp
(16)
(16)
(17)
(18)
poco rall.

1. This is rushed.
2. The upper note is actually an E♭.
3. This chord also contains a B♭.
4. The lower pitch is actually an F.
5. The line above is a simpler version of the highly ornamented line Morton actually plays.
6. The highest note is actually an F.
7. This is partly conjectural. What Morton plays is not clear.
8. A C sounds with the B♮.
9. The upper note is actually not present.
10. The two pitches are not attacked precisely together.
11. Morton does not actually play this octave.
12. This A♮ in this interval is played very quietly.
13. The four measures beginning with measure 25 are more rhythmically fluid, and many of the pitches sustained longer, than the notation indicates.
14. Morton actually plays an E♮.
15. A D sounds with the C.
16. Following a pattern which he often uses elsewhere, Morton actually plays A♮ here.
17. An A♭ above the G also sounds.
18. An A♭ also sounds with the B♭.

SPANISH SWAT

COPYRIGHT:

Not copyrighted during Morton's lifetime.

RECORDING:

*May 21-July, 1938: piano solo, recorded (1685) in the Library of Congress by Alan Lomax; ♩ = c. 106 increasing to c. 126.

Spanish Swat, whose only recorded performance by Morton is transcribed here, is a distinctly small-scale "Spanish tinge*" piece. It is unique among the pieces in this volume for its having only one strain*, a thirty-two-measure AABA structure—an atypical one for Morton—with each section eight measures in length. (The uniqueness of this single-strain format, and the lack of variety which that causes, raises the possibility that this could be only part of a piece, perhaps part of an unfinished one.)

The outline of the performance is also unusual. Morton plays a first, unornamented chorus*, then an improvised variation on it. Next, perhaps to avoid a too-repetitive performance, he plays four [b]'s, four bridges*, then returns to the full chorus to end. The disc's running out prevented the recording of the last eight measures of the chorus, but this edition provides a version of the missing last eight measures based on what Morton had played earlier in the performance. In the performance Morton probably also played a longer introduction than is notated here, but the recording captured only the last three beats of it.

Spanish Swat

"Jelly Roll" Morton

Spanish Swat

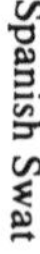

[Chorus 2]

3
9
(5)
17
18
19
20
21
22
23
24
25
26
27
28
29
30
31
32

[b1]
3
1 2 3 4
5 6 7
[b2]
8 1 2
3 4 5
6 7 8

[b3]
[b4]
(6)

[Chorus 3]
(7)

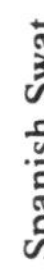
Spanish Swat

1. The B♭ is actually not present.
2. The chord also contains a B♭ below middle C.
3. Morton also plays a D♭ above middle C in this chord.
4. Morton strikes a C with the D♮.
5. The low C is faint.
6. Morton actually plays an A♮, not an A♭, in the group of thirty-second notes.
7. The lower F is not actually present.
8. This is the point at which the disc ended.

THE PEARLS

COPYRIGHT:

August 20, 1923: piano solo version, Morton holograph; Melrose Brothers Music Company,
April 1, 1925: orchestration; Melrose Brothers Music Company.

RECORDINGS:

+July 18, 1923: piano solo; Gennett 5323 (11547); ♩ = c. 153,
+April 20, 1926: piano solo; Vocalion 1020 (C-160); ♩ = c. 170 increasing to c. 178,
June 10, 1927: Jelly-Roll Morton's Red Hot Peppers; Victor 20948 (38662-3); ♩ = c. 150,
+May 21-July, 1938: piano solo, recorded (1677) in the Library of Congress by Alan Lomax; ♩ = c. 138 increasing to c. 149,
*c. August, 1938: piano solo, private recording subsequently issued commercially (Swaggie JCS-116 and S-1213); ♩ = c. 140 increasing to c. 143.

The Pearls, an elegant, large-scale three-strain* piece, is deservedly one of the most widely admired Morton works.

This 1919 composition was dedicated to a waitress at the Kansas City Bar in Tijuana. Morton explained the title by saying that the piece consisted of several sections, "each one matching the other and contributing to the total effect of a beautiful pearl necklace."[1] He went on to describe it as one of his two most difficult compositions to perform.

[1]Alan Lomax, *Mr. Jelly Roll* (New York: Duell, Sloane and Pearce, 1950).

Like many of Morton's other pieces, *The Pearls* is built upon contrast, rather than upon interrelationship, its form dependent upon the balance of its parts. In identifying *The Pearls* in particular as more difficult to play than many other pieces requiring greater technical facility and stamina, Morton shows the depth of his musical judgment: he is referring not to "mere" technical difficulty, but to the artistic task of drawing together the piece's diverse elements into a coherent whole.

Each of the first two sixteen-measure strains is distinctive, the first with its colorful harmony and composed break*, and the second with its deliberately simpler basic harmonic outline, complicated and dissonant right-hand part, and break placed near the end. (And also—not a composed part of the piece—the left-hand parallel tenths which Morton used on this and his other 1938 recording of the piece.) They set a level of complexity and detail which only a still-richer third strain will balance.

Morton's third strain is perfect in satisfying this need. Its new left-hand pattern, arresting in itself, is the basis for some of the phrasing manipulation he uses. The left hand's alternation of C and G sounds at first as if it were a two-measure vamp, but as the strain progresses and the length and placement of the melodic phrases above readjust themselves it becomes, almost in retrospect, a part of the sixteen measures of the first half of the strain.

The first melodic phrase consists of a pickup figure—in measure 2—and the phrase's cadence in measure 3. In a general way the phrasing marks in the edition show what happens to this pattern: the pickup gestures start earlier relative to the eventual cadence and increase the total phrase length. After a phrase which readjusts the scheme (mm. 8 and 9), the pickups begin in odd-numbered measures (mm. 9 and 11) for two phrases. Once this new scheme (odd to even rather than even to odd) has been established, a lengthy reference to the dominant key of G major, the key of the first two strains, appears and brings the first half of the strain to a solid-textured close.

The solo reappearance of the left hand—an interruption which presents one of the difficulties in holding the performance together because it appears every sixteen measures—makes the second half of the strain sound as if it were to proceed in the same way. But a new and longer phrase appears (m. 20), moving harmonically to the subdominant, and from there the strain is more regularly phrased. This regularity and the solidly cadence-directed harmony coincide to produce a strong conclusion to the strain.

Here again a performance shows Morton's disciplined improvising: his phrasing in the variations on the third strain correspond almost exactly to the composed phrasing, the changes being, characteristically for Morton's improvising, lengthening of phrases and eliding them together into longer ones.

The Pearls

"Jelly Roll" Morton

tr
(3)

[A1 - 2]
(4)
tr
tr

[B - 1]

[B - 2]

[A2]
(6)
(7)
tr
tr
(8)
tr
tr

[Transition]

tr

12 12

1 2 3

8

12

[C - 1]

4 1 2 3

4 5 6 7

8 9 10 11

12 13 14

[C - 2]

17 18 19

20 21 22

23 24 25

26 27 28

29 30 31 32 *tr*

[C - 3]

Morton's four recordings of *The Pearls* show an interesting evolution in his conception of the piece. Several examples from other versions are transcribed below.

The Library of Congress recording of *The Pearls* is nearly contemporaneous with the August 1938 recording transcribed fully above. The introduction of the slightly later recording, transcribed below, is somewhat better played and is connected more smoothly with the first strain.

On both of his earlier recordings and in his own notation, Morton's original version of the second strain was somewhat simpler than the one he used in 1938. A transcription of the Gennett version's second strain is shown below.

Morton's Vocalion performance presents a unique way of playing the first statement of the third strain, transcribed below. Here Morton uses a left-hand style which he used often in other pieces but which appears in no other recording of this piece. To introduce this novel way of playing the piece, Morton improvises an attractive, syncopated left-hand figure in the first two measures of the strain.

[C - 1] from Vocalion performance

(11)
cresc.

The Library of Congress recording is similar to the complete version transcribed above. The most interesting difference is in Morton's performance of third-strain variations. Below are transcribed the last three, of five, choruses on the third strain. They show, unlike other performances, the use of the stride-like left-hand style.

mf
cresc.
(13)
f

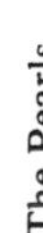

[C - 4]

(14) (14)

dim.

(15)

mf
(16)
(17)
(18)
(19)

[C - 5]
(20)
tr

On his earlier solo recording, his band recording, and in his manuscript, Morton used the composed ending shown below, transcribed from the Gennett recording. The ending is a pun, sounding, after a full close of a third-strain chorus, as if still another chorus were beginning. For the later recordings Morton abandoned this ending in favor of a more characteristic four-measure ending, one probably better in keeping with the scale of the piece as a whole.

[Ending] from Gennett recording

1. This is what Morton is likely to have played. The recording here is not clear.
2. Morton actually plays the G a fourth higher.
3. Morton may have meant to play a tenth here, with the middle C above the A.
4. Morton actually played a tenth here with the higher B and the G a tenth below.
5. The upper pitch is actually an A.
6. The lower pitch is actually an A a second above the written G.
7. The upper pitch is actually a B♮, not a C♯.
8. Morton actually plays an A a second above the written G.
9. Morton actually plays a very quiet D above middle C rather than this F♯.
10. An A above the G also sounds.
11. A G below the A also sounds.
12. An A below the B also sounds.
13. This two-measure span is very difficult to hear. Morton may have played more than is indicated here.
14. These chords also contain B♭'s below the middle C, a mistake.
15. Morton actually played a D octave a second below.
16. The rhythm of this measure, and of the previous two, is somewhat less precise than the notation indicates.
17. With the B and D Morton also plays an F. Although these pitches can be seen as anticipations of pitches of the harmony next to appear, it is likely that Morton would have preferred to play a C♯ or C♯ and G, as he did in other performances of this measure.
18. Here, too, Morton anticipates harmonies which appear later. He would probably have preferred to play an F♯ instead of the F and C♮ instead of B.
19. Morton may not have intended to play the B's in these chords.
20. Morton may have meant to play a B rather than the A between D and F.
21. Morton actually plays: 
22. Morton actually plays F's, not E's, in these chords.
23. There is a G below, or instead of, the higher A.

FINGERBUSTER
also known as FINGERBREAKER

COPYRIGHT:

Not copyrighted during Morton's lifetime.

RECORDING:

*December, 1938: piano solo, Jazz Man 12 (MLB-145); ♩ = c. 277 increasing to c. 305.

According to Morton, *Fingerbuster* is "the most difficult piece of jazz piano ever written."[1] Whether or not this is true, it certainly moves at breakneck speed and is dazzling in its effect and momentum. With the possible exception of *Perfect Rag,* it might well be the most technically demanding piece in this volume.

As often happens with virtuoso pieces, this work's function as a display piece results in its purely musical values being overshadowed. Some of the ideas in the piece are similar to ideas Morton used elsewhere, and, in some of those cases, to better advantage.

Much about this piece suggests the possibility of a considerably earlier origin for it than 1938. The first strain, up to measure 16, could pass for an improvisation on the first strain* of *Frog-I-More Rag.* At that point Morton continues with what is probably the least distinctive and least effective segment of the piece. He adds sixteen measures whose construction lengthens the first strain to thirty-two measures, making this the only known first strain of such length in Morton's music. The second half of the first strain, with the return of the music used in the first and second eight-measure phrases to become the last eight measures, gives the strain an AABA shape, something atypical of Morton's thirty-two-measure strains. When Morton returns to the first strain after playing the second, he plays only the first half of it. The abbreviation may have been made for reasons of time economy on the recording, but it also actually improves the strain.

[1]Lomax, *op. cit.*

The second strain, reminiscent of that of *Perfect Rag,* is simple, but more concentrated and more effective.

Also like *Perfect Rag,* another overtly virtuoso piece, *Fingerbuster* has a sixteen-measure third strain, which is probably the best one, with Morton features of a strong bass line in counterpoint with the melody. Morton's improvising on this strain is not "serious" in the sense that his playing of his major pieces is, but even with the essentially textural—that is, unmelodic—approach he uses, he creates five consecutive choruses* which build very effectively toward the end of the performance.

Finger Buster

"Jelly Roll" Morton

26 27 28

29 30 31 32

[A^1 - 2]

1 2 3 4

5 6 7 8

9 10 11 12

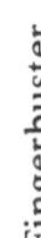

13
14
15
16
17
18
19
(4)
20
21
22
23
24
25
26
27
28
29
30
31
32

[B - 1]

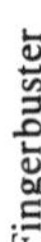

456

[B - 2]

[A2]
1
2
3
4
5
6
7
8
9
10
11
12
13
14
15
16

[Transition]
(7)
[C -1]
(8)
(9)
(10)
(11)
(12)

[C - 2]

(13)

(14)

[C - 3]
(8)
(15)
(16)
3

[C - 4]

[C - 5]

1. Morton actually plays an F.
2. Morton does not actually play the G♭.
3. A G also sounds in this chord.
4. Morton actually plays the F a second below.
5. Morton actually plays an A octave a second below.
6. Morton actually plays a single A a second below.
7. The middle pitch is actually a D.
8. Morton actually plays a B♭ dominant seventh chord as in the left hand's second and fourth beats of the previous measure.
9. Morton actually plays an E♭ major chord as on the second beat of the next measure.
10. A middle C also sounds.
11. Morton plays the notated G and an E♭ and an A♮ below it.
12. A B♮ below the high C also sounds.
13. This is rushed.
14. Morton actually plays a C octave a second below.
15. The upper note is actually an A♮.
16. Morton actually plays a B♭ dominant seventh chord as on the fourth beat of the previous measure.
17. Morton also plays a D a second above the C.
18. The upper note is actually A♮.
19. A C♯ below the upper D also sounds.
20. A D above the lower C also sounds.

HONKY TONK MUSIC

COPYRIGHT:

Not copyrighted during Morton's lifetime.

RECORDING:

*December, 1938: piano solo; Jazz Man 11 (MLB-149); ♩ = c. 115 increasing to c. 130.

Morton's few boogie-woogie recordings are appealing and *Honky Tonk Music* is the only piece in this volume truly in a boogie-woogie style. (*Jungle Blues,* a carefully worked-out composition, uses a similar left-hand pattern, but it is not an improvised blues* as most "authentic" boogie-woogie pieces are.) In *Mr. Jelly Roll,* Alan Lomax states that this solo recording and the one of *Fingerbuster* date from an abortive band-recording session in Washington, suggesting that Morton was not prepared to make solo recordings. Indeed it might well be that Morton merely worked out *Honky Tonk Music* on the spot.

The formal outline of the piece is simple: there are two blues choruses*, two sixteen-measure choruses in the relative minor—the first a "Spanish tinge*" chorus and the second using another conventional boogie-woogie left-hand pattern—then two more blues choruses in the tonic recalling the first blues choruses. The differentiation between the pairs of blues choruses and the use of the "Spanish tinge" chorus between show Morton's response to the necessity of making a real composition out of very simple material.

Morton most often used the "Spanish tinge" for very refined pieces, but included it here in a piece the rest of whose style and title hardly allude to refinement. It is clear from some of Morton's Library of Congress material, from pieces by other composers—*St. Louis Blues* and *Memphis Blues* by W. C. Handy, for instance—and from such other pieces as Morton's own *New Orleans Blues,* that the "Spanish tinge" also has a traditional place in jazz's basic blues sources.

Honky Tonk Music

"Jelly Roll" Morton

466

(2)
10
11
12
[A^{1}-2]
(3)
1
2
3
4
5
6
7
8
9
10
11
12

[B1]
tr

[B2]
(4)
(5)
8

* Simultaneous grace note.

tr
[C-2]
(7)
(8)

1. Throughout, when using this left-hand figure, Morton introduces variations in its articulation. The variations are similar to those he uses in performing the same figure in ***Jungle Blues*** (q.v.).
2. The lower F is actually not present.
3. Morton begins this chorus by playing all eighth notes swung but switches to even eighth notes in both hands by measure 4. Once the chorus is over, he reverts to swung eighth notes throughout.
4. A B♮ below the C also sounds.
5. An A above the G also sounds.
6. The recording is unclear here. This solution is conjectural.
7. The upper note is actually a C a second below the written D.
8. The pitch between the A's, G's, and F's is actually an E♭.

THE CRAVE

COPYRIGHT:

December 20, 1939: lead sheet*, Morton holograph; Tempo-Music Publishing Company.

RECORDINGS:

+May 21-July, 1938: piano solo, recorded (master number unknown) in the Library of Congress by Alan Lomax; ♩ = c. 138 increasing to c. 143,
*December 14, 1939: piano solo; General 4003 (R-2562); ♩ = c. 148.

The Crave is one of Morton's extended "Spanish tinge"* compositions, a piece of unusual beauty, with elegant long lines, effectively devised and placed textural variety, and a fine, strong ending. It first appears in Morton's recorded output in 1938 but was probably composed much earlier.

Thornton Hagert of Vernacular Music Research has discovered that *The Crave,* like Sidney Bechet's *Egyptian Fantasy,* is partly derived from Abe Olman's *Egyptia,* which was published in 1911 in Chicago by Will Rossiter, Morton's first publisher. The conjunction of time, place, and publisher—Morton was playing at the Deluxe and the Elite Cafe #1 in Chicago at times between 1910 and 1915—of course also brings up the possibility that Olman's piece is based on Morton's rather than the reverse.

(Charles Edward Smith's notes[1] for the set of records for which this performance was recorded, General Records' "Jelly Roll Morton's New Orleans Memories," makes the claim that "There is not a tune in this album that wasn't played in New Orleans before 1910..." In saying this, and in claiming that Morton had played the piece at Hillma *(sic)* Burt's sporting house, Smith might have been quoting or paraphrasing Morton, whose statements about dates were not always accurate.)

[1]Charles Edward Smith, accompanying notes for the record album "Jelly Roll Morton's New Orleans Memories," copyright (no date) by General Records Division, Consolidated Records, Inc.

Bechet's piece merely states *Egyptia*'s first two strains* in undisguised form and omits the third. *The Crave* uses the harmonic pattern of Olman's first strain —which does not use the tango or habañera rhythm—and a few similar melodic gestures, notably the stereotyped "Spanish" gesture in octaves which concludes the strain, then proceeds to two original strains. (Olman's and Morton's second strains resemble each other in containing breaks* and in some details of harmony too.) *The Crave* and *Egyptia* have nothing in common in their third strains.

The second-strain tonality of F major and single statement in this performance give it the quality of a mere connective section between two more important strains, even despite its beauty and textural interest. (This single statement of the second strain and the absence of return of the first strain are apparently not a part of the piece's conception, for when Morton made his Library of Congress recording of *The Crave* he did repeat the second strain and then restate the first before arriving at the third.)

In outline—main harmonic pattern, placement of breaks, and in their two different halves—the third strains of *The Crave* and *Creepy Feeling* resemble each other. In detail, however, they are quite different: where *Creepy Feeling* refers tonally back to the piece's second strain in measures 13 to 16, *The Crave* refers back to the first strain (that is, it refers to D minor). In measures 13 to 16 Morton strongly recalls the first strain not only tonally but in texture and melody too, particularly in the use of the "Spanish" gesture in measure 15. This is especially tellingly placed because it is immediately followed by the parallel-octave gesture native to the third strain itself, introducing the beautiful and unexpected second half of the strain, with a new melody beginning in measure 17. In *Creepy Feeling* Morton at this point continued the melodic style set earlier in the piece, not—as he does here—making this point the focus for everything that had happened previously in the piece.

The Crave

"Jelly Roll" Morton

* Simultaneous grace note

* Simultaneous grace note

[C - 1]
mf
tr
f
(5)
mf
f
(6)
(7)
(8)
mf

L.H.
(9)
(10)

[C - 2]
L.H.
tr
(11)
(12)

Morton's repetition of the first strain as [A²] on his Library of Congress recording changes the shape of the piece but also shows the strain itself in a slightly different light, with a unique left-hand style. It is transcribed below.

1. A G a second below the higher A also sounds.
2. A C a second below the higher D also sounds.
3. An E is sounded with the D, and held after the D is released.
4. An E a second below the F also sounds.
5. An F a second below the upper G also sounds.
6. A G♮ below the lower G♯ also sounds.
7. A G a second below the lower A also sounds.
8. The lower note is actually F above middle C.
9. The upper note is actually A a second above the written higher G.
10. The upper note is actually B♭ a second above the higher A.
11. A D sounds with the E♮.
12. A C♯ a second below the higher D also sounds.
13. An E between the F's also sounds.
14. A B♮ between the C's also sounds.

MISTER JOE
originally recorded as BUFFALO BLUES

COPYRIGHT:

April 2, 1928 (as *Buffalo Blues*): lead sheet*, Morton holograph; Triangle Music Publishing Company,
September 26, 1939: lead sheet*, Morton holograph; Tempo-Music Publishing Company.

RECORDINGS:

March 13, 1928 (as *Buffalo Blues*): Johnny Dunn and His Band with Morton, piano; Columbia 14358-D (145760-1); ♩ = c. 126 decreasing to c. 118,
December 14, 1939: piano solo; General 4004 (R-2564); ♩ = c. 149 increasing to c. 151.

Mister Joe is a fine, even piece containing multiple uses of one of Morton's favorite harmonic patterns, and is designed to be played at the medium tempo Morton used so effectively. The quality of evenness comes from the work's deemphasis of textural contrast, the fact that all of its strains are of the same length, and the similarity of the first and third strains.

The introduction and ending are made from the last four measures of the first strain, one whose harmonic pattern—or at least the first eight measures of it—Morton had used often in other pieces. The melody's insistent repeated gesture sets a pattern for the entire piece by emphasizing the two-measure phrase length which is used throughout the composition.

The principal element of contrast in the piece is in the second strain with its harmonic and melodic sequence moving through a cycle of fifths to reach the tonic at the break in measure 7. The four-measure ending phrase reappears later as the last four measures of the third strain. (Morton's improvised chorus, [B-2], uses an ending closer to that of the first strain, something Morton might not have planned to do.)

The third strain is an interesting combination of the first—using the harmonic pattern of its first twelve measures—and the second—using the entire four-measure ending phrase. In addition it introduces a new melodic element, the accented B-natural to C movement which appears—as the lowest notes in the right hand—at the beginning of every odd-numbered measure until the ending phrase. Morton improvises answering phrases between the statements of this fixed element, a kind of division of right-hand activity he used many times and in as early a piece as *King Porter Stomp.* In his variation on the strain Morton's improvised answers become more overtly melodic, and one can only wish that there had been time for him to play two or three more choruses to carry this idea further, as he was able to do with some of the pieces he recorded in the Library of Congress.

Mister Joe was first recorded, under its earlier title of *Buffalo Blues,* in a band version during Morton's first New York recording session, one in which he played with, and probably directed, the Johnny Dunn band. Charles Edward Smith's notes for the solo recording transcribed here state that the piece was also played by the King Oliver band. Considering the Oliver band's recordings of *London Blues* and *Froggie Moore,* the latter never even published, it seems possible that this piece was, as Smith said, "... one of the favorite numbers of Joe Oliver's Creole Jazz Band."[1]

[1]Smith, *op. cit.*

Mister Joe

[B - 1]

[B - 2]
tr
(4)
(5)
(6)
3

[A^2]

[Transition]

[C -1]

mf sfz

sfz

sfz

sfz

sfz

tr

(7)

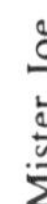

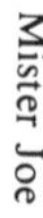

[C - 2]

(8)

(9)

(10)

[Coda]

1. The inner notes between the G's are actually E♭'s a second higher.
2. The upper note is actually B♮.
3. The note between the G's is actually an E♭.
4. A B♮ also sounds above the A, and the rhythm is perhaps closer to [rhythm: eighth note followed by an eighth-note triplet (3)].
5. Between the D and F Morton also plays a B♭.
6. A D between the two E♮'s also sounds.
7. The upper note is actually a faintly played D♭.
8. The upper note is actually not present.
9. Morton actually plays an E♭ major chord with B♭ below middle C and the E♭ and G above.
10. Morton actually plays an octave F a second lower.

KING PORTER STOMP

COPYRIGHT:

December 9, 1924: orchestration; Melrose Brothers Music Company.

RECORDINGS:

July 17, 1923: piano solo; Gennett 5289 (11537); ♩ = c. 187 increasing to c. 196,
December, 1924: King Oliver, cornet solo with Morton, piano; Autograph 617 (685); ♩ = c. 190 increasing to c. 201,
1924: piano roll; Vocalstyle 50480,
April 20, 1926: piano solo; Vocalion 1020 (C-166); ♩ = c. 168 increasing to c. 189,
May 21-July, 1938: two piano solo versions, recorded (1639, 1674) in the Library of Congress by Alan Lomax; ♩ = c. 193 increasing to c. 243; and ♩ = c. 166 increasing to c. 168,
*December 14, 1939: piano solo; General 4005 (R-2565); ♩ = c. 183 increasing to c. 185,
July 14, 1940: piano solo with Nat Levine, drums; recorded from "NBC Chamber Music Society of Lower Basin Street" radio broadcast; ♩ = c. 197 increasing to c. 219.

King Porter Stomp is a fitting last piece for this volume, one of Morton's best works and perhaps his best known, a composition important to Morton and to jazz in general. The piece is warm and robust, full of the vitality that is characteristic of Morton at his best.

Morton himself made more recordings of this composition—including his first and last known solo recordings—than of any of his others, and during his life it was recorded commercially about twenty times by others. Several of these recordings were made when the piece was first published, then later, in the late 1930s, more recordings of it were made by Claude Hopkins, Benny Goodman, Harry James, the Metronome All-Stars, and others. Aside from this, *King Porter Stomp* is important for its influence on other pieces.

Morton wrote *King Porter Stomp* in 1906 while in Memphis, and named it for his friend, pianist Porter King. Blesh and Janis suggest that parts of the composition may actually have been composed by King. Their suggestion that the piece was copyrighted in 1906 is not borne out by copyright records.

King Porter Stomp's three strains—always played in order, with no return to the first after the second, an atypical Morton scheme—show several characteristic tendencies in Morton's music.

The first places its exceptional texture—the absence of the stridelike left hand—at the beginning of the strain. It also shows a harmonic sophistication in its use, in measures 3 and 4, of a supertonic rather than dominant of the dominant chord (a difference in this case between using a D♮ and a D♭). This is an apparently small difference between two similarly functioning harmonies, but is one which makes an expressive difference in giving a more restrained, less brilliant, harmonic effect.

The second strain, with a composed break in measures 7 and 8, is one of the most ragtime-styled of Morton's ideas and, perhaps for that reason, is the part usually omitted in later band performances of the piece.

One of Morton's most forward-looking creations is his third strain of *King Porter Stomp.* He used its riff-type construction in many other pieces, but in this piece his composed variations pointed the way for arrangers and composers for years to come: his full-voiced right-hand chords suggested a full band, and his division of the right-hand music into question-and-answer statements (as in [C-3] and [C-4]) suggested division of the band into sections.

This is altogether a good performance, superior in its balance of Morton the composer and Morton the performer to any of the other six performances of the piece, with each strain well carried out and the whole performance beautifully shaped. The playing of the third strain's statements is especially fine: the first is calm and full-voiced; the second is expanded in range, activity, and amount of syncopation; the third is still more active, with the right-hand phrases short and incisive and beginning to suggest division among the band's sections; the fourth, only a partial chorus, actively separates the right-hand music by both gesture and register and proceeds to a typically intense and climactic ending.

King Porter Stomp

[A - 2]
(1)
(2)
(3)
(4)
(5)

[B - 1]
1
2
3
4
5
6
7
8
9
10
11
12
13
14
15
16
(6)

[B - 2]
(7)
(8)
(9)
(10) (11)
tr

[Transition]

[C - 1]

mp *cresc.*

mf

[C - 2]
1
2
3
4
5
6
7
8
9
10
11
12
13
14
15
16
(12)

[C - 3]
mp
mf
mp
mf
cresc.
f
mf
cresc.

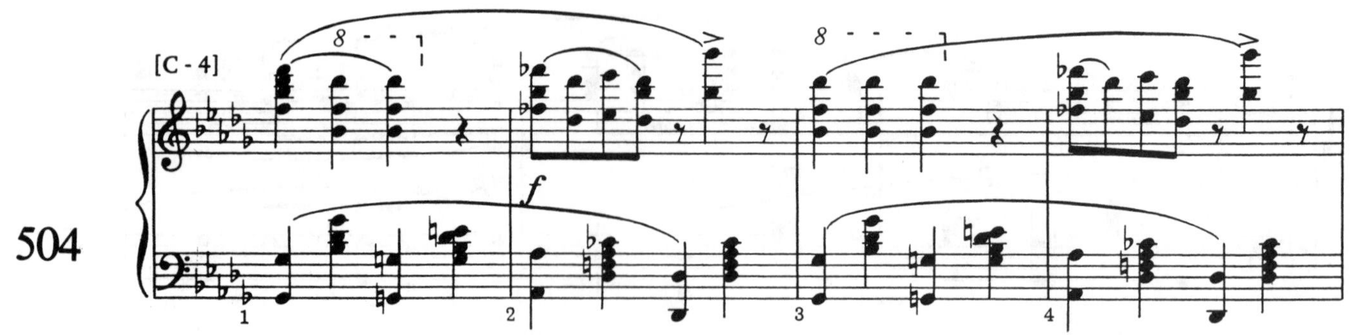
[C - 4]
8
f
1
2
3
4

8
5
6
7
6

dim.
mf
(13)
9
10
11
12

1. This chord also contains a D♭ above middle C.
2. Morton actually plays an A♭ a second lower.
3. This B♭ appears slightly earlier than the notation indicates.
4. The D♭ is not present or very faint.
5. The lower pitch in each of these intervals is actually an E♭ above middle C.
6. A D♮ between the E♮'s also sounds.
7. The lowest note is faint.
8. An F below the lower G also sounds.
9. The lower G is not actually present.
10. The lower note is actually a D♮.
11. The lower note is actually not present.
12. The upper pitch is actually an E♭.
13. The chord also contains a G♮.

GLOSSARY

GLOSSARY

Blues. In its most widely used technical meaning, a twelve-measure strain with a harmonic outline in which the tonic harmony appears in the first measure, the subdominant in the fifth, the tonic in the seventh, the dominant in the ninth or tenth and the tonic in the eleventh. I.e.:

‖I | | | |IV | |I | |(V) |(V) |I | ‖

Measure 1 3 5 7 9 11

This basic outline accommodates the vast majority of blues of most periods. The exceptions are often the result of (1) substituting harmonies with the same or similar function (such as the mediant for the tonic in m. 7 found in many modern blues), (2) somewhat delaying the appearance of a harmony (such as maintaining the subdominant in m. 7 and moving to the tonic in m. 8, as in the traditional *Frankie and Johnny* and in Duke Ellington's *Creole Love Call),* and (3) a kind of deceptive cadence procedure in which the final appearance of the tonic in m. 11 may be delayed by a brief reappearance of the subdominant. The great variety of blues is the result of the variety of ways in which the basic harmonies diagrammed above are approached and played as shown or delayed.

Break. A span of time, usually two measures, during which explicit statement of the pulse, *not* the pulse itself, is suspended. (In Morton's solo playing this was accomplished by his stopping the stridelike left hand. In band performances the rhythm section rests.) The term is also used to denote the music played during the suspension of the statement of the pulse.

Bridge. The *b* section in popular music and jazz strains of sixteen measures or thirty-two-measures, when the phrases (four or eight measures) can be symbolized *a a b a,* the principal element of contrast. (The third strain of *Seattle Hunch* is the type of chorus structure which has a bridge.)

Chase chorus. A chorus so divided that alternate segments, of usually two or four measures, are played by different improvising players, usually two. When this alternating is done with four-measure segments, the routine is called "taking fours."

Chorus. 1. A complete statement of a strain (q.v.); 2. An improvised solo lasting one chorus as defined in 1; 3. In popular music and jazz, the principal strain, the one by which the piece is known, in contrast to the verse (q.v.), which in importance is the secondary strain.

Double-time. A tempo twice as fast as the one established as the basic one for performance. Most often, when using double-time, musicians play twice as many measures in double-time as they would have played at the normal tempo, making the total elapsed time the same as it would normally have been. Morton used double-time in the performance of *Mr. Jelly Lord,* transcribed in this volume.

Four-bar ending. An ending phrase which begins in the penultimate measure of the chorus and extends for two measures beyond the full length of the chorus, usually prolonging the tonic harmony. A four-bar ending in a thirty-two-measure chorus then begins in m. 31 and appears to extend the chorus to a length of 34 measures (as in the last chorus of *Wolverine Blues* in this volume. A thirty-two-measure chorus with a "normal" ending is used as the last chorus of *Shreveport Stomp*). The extension is then only two measures long, the last two measures of the chorus not disappearing but playing a double role.

Ghost notes. Very quietly played notes, almost always pitches basic to the prevailing harmony, which precede strongly attacked principal pitches of a melody. Their function seems to be rhythmic, to impart an additional element of swing, and to prepare for the attacks following. The practice may have originated in ragtime's figuration, as jazz musicians' performances of ragtime suggest.

Lead sheet. The simplest possible notation of a piece, often no more than the melody, sometimes with the harmonies and/or lyrics also represented. Many copyright deposits of Morton's compositions are lead sheets rather than more nearly complete notations such as sheet music, piano versions, or orchestrations.

"Modern." For a time an adjective with a technical—rather than stylistic—meaning, denoting the kind of experimentally chromatic use of harmony found in parts of *Freakish,* James P. Johnson's *You've Got To Be Modernistic,* and Eubie Blake's *Dictys on 7th Avenue,* among other pieces. "Modern" harmony usually exploits the effect of cross-relations.

Riff. 1. In its original and commonest meaning, a repeated melodic figure, usually short, often used as an accompaniment. Through its repetitions a riff gains a kind of momentum which in the melodic aspect of a piece is rather like swing in the rhythmic and metric aspect. Parts of many of Morton's pieces are rifflike, with construction in repeated two-measure melodic and harmonic units. *King Porter Stomp*'s third strain gives a famous example of such construction. 2. An idea, usually brief, which is identifiable without repetition. In this sense it is synonymous with the dated term "lick." Morton, in speaking on the Library of Congress recordings, used this term in both senses.

"Spanish tinge." Morton referred to his pieces with the tango or habañera rhythm in the left hand as having the Spanish tinge. The rhythm is more related to jazz's African antecedents than it is to the Spanish influence on jazz.

Stride. A piano style, strongly rooted in ragtime, associated with James P. Johnson, Fats Waller, and others. The left-hand technique, only a part of what defines stride, involves the use of a lower-register single note, octave, tenth, or other interval on the first and third beats of the (four-four) measure and middle-register chords on the second and fourth beats, the function being the statement of both pulse and harmony. This left-hand style was used in ragtime and, in various incarnations, by jazz pianists well into the 1940s. Stride is only one of many styles—including those of Morton, Earl Hines, Art Tatum, etc.—which use this left-hand technique but it is the only style with a generally understood name. Hence the use of the term "stridelike" here even though, considering the range of features which define stride, Morton was not a stride pianist, and even though stride style does not necessarily have historical, or any other, primacy over Morton's or other pianists' styles.

Strain. A complete musical unit, usually eight, twelve, sixteen, or thirty-two measures in length (though pieces in this volume also contain strains fourteen, twenty and twenty-two measures long). The distinction between strain and chorus is that the word "strain" carries with it the recognition of a certain content or musical identity, and the word "chorus" refers only to a single complete strain statement. Thus, in representing a performance with letters to indicate strains, I have used the symbols A^1; B; A^2; C-1; C-2 to mean that there are three strains (three musical entities, A, B, and C) and five choruses (five complete statements of strains). One can also say that there are two consecutive choruses of, or on, the third strain.

Swing. The propulsive, rhythmic quality of jazz when properly played. Conceptions of swing are not entirely fixed in jazz—though the necessity for its presence seems to be—but have changed periodically, within a fairly narrow range, sometimes reinstating previously discarded conceptions.

Swung. When referring to eighth notes, the uneven long-short quality of pairs of eighth notes played during one beat, an essential ingredient of swing.

Vamp. A short segment of music designed to establish or reestablish a key, and sometimes to provide rest before a performer, usually a singer, begins. A vamp is usually modular in its construction—a two-measure phrase ending on the dominant harmony is a typical module—so that it can be repeated to make any length necessary at the moment. *Midnight Mama* has a vamp immediately after its introduction. Its purpose is to establish the key of B♭ major after the introduction in F, the main key of the piece.

Verse. The part of a popular music or jazz piece which is usually less well known—if it is known at all—and often less melodic. Its lyrics, especially in show music, are introductory or primarily expository. In that sense, as well as in the fact that it can be of irregular length and is often performed rubato, it is somewhat similar to a recitative preceding an aria, the aria being represented by the chorus.

BIBLIOGRAPHY

Allen, Walter C. *King Joe Oliver.* London: Sidgwick and Jackson, 1958.

Anonymous. "Success of 'Jelly Roll' Morton Number Prompts Melrose Bros. to Launch Folio," *The Music Trades,* February 4, 1924.

Barr, Steven C. *The (Almost) Complete 78rpm Record Dating Guide.* Toronto, 1979.

Blesh, Rudi, and Harriet Janis. *They All Played Ragtime.* New York: Grove Press, 1950.

Charters, Samuel B. *Jazz: New Orleans, 1885–1963.* Rev. ed. New York: Oak Publications, 1963.

Chilton, John. *Who's Who In Jazz.* London: Bloomsbury Book Shop, 1970.

Davis, John R. T., and Laurie Wright. *Morton's Music.* London: Storyville Publications and Co., 1968.

Hulsizer, Kenneth. "Jelly Roll Morton in Washington," *Jazz Music.* February-March, 1944.

Kramer, Karl. "Jelly Roll in Chicago; the Missing Chapter," *The Ragtimer.* April, 1967.

Lomax, Alan. *Mr. Jelly Roll.* New York: Grove Press, 1950.

Miller, Paul Eduard, ed. *Esquire's 1946 Jazz Book.* New York: A. S. Barnes and Co., 1946.

Montgomery, Mike. "Piano Roll Notes: More Rolls by Morton," *Record Research.* March, 1963.

Morton, Jelly Roll. "Fragment of an Autobiography," Part 1, *The Jazz Record.* March, 1944. Part 2, April, 1944.

Morton, Jelly Roll. "I Created Jazz in 1902," *The Jazz Record.* April, 1945. (Reprint of a letter sent to, and published by, *Down Beat* magazine in 1938.)

Rust, Brian. *Jazz Records 1897–1942.* 4th ed. New York: Arlington House, 1978.

Schuller, Gunther. *Early Jazz.* New York: Oxford University Press, 1968.

Simeon, Omer. "Mostly About Morton," *The Jazz Record.* October, 1945.

Smith, Charles Edward. *Jelly Roll Morton's New Orleans Memories.* New York: 1939(?). (Booklet to accompany the General record album of the same title.)

Smith, Charles Edward. "Oh, Mr. Jelly!" *The Jazz Record.* February, 1944.

Smith, Harrison. "Debunking Jelly Roll," *Record Research.* June-July, 1957.

Smith, Harrison. "The 'Fableous' Jelly Roll," *Record Research.* January-February, 1957.

Smith, Harrison. "Jelly Roll's Strange Will," *Record Research.* October, 1961.

Smith, Harrison. "Malice in Blunderland," *Record Research.* January, 1962.

Smith, Harrison. "Some Jelly Roll Morton Vignettes," *Record Research.* October, 1960.

Valenti, Jerry. "Jelly Roll Morton and the Library of Congress," *The Jazz Record.* March, 1946.

Williams, Martin. *Jelly Roll Morton.* New York: A. S. Barnes and Co., 1963.

Williams, Martin. Liner notes for *Jelly Roll Morton: Library of Congress Recordings.* New York: Riverside Records, Nos. 9001 to 9012, 1957.